Joshua,
Connec
Cross in Love !

Robert E. Lee's Orderly

A Modern Black Man's Confederate Journey
Extended Edition

By Al Arnold

3/7/20

Robert E. Lee's Orderly
A Modern Black Man's Confederate Journey
Extended Edition

© 2018 Al Arnold

Cover art and illustrations by
Gregory Newson, Newson Publishing
Newsonpublishing.com
Newburgh NY

Cover Design
Diana Thornton, Crescent Music Services
Crescentmusic.com
New Orleans, LA 70119

ISBN 13: 978-0-692-16257-6

ISBN 10: 0-692-16257-7

Contents

Al Arnold is one brave man. I have found him to be a man of great principle. I frequently attend the Multi Ethnic Church that he attends in Jackson, Mississippi. We occasionally participate in the same Sunday School Class. Though I don't agree with all of his views, he certainly challenges the heart and soul of a man to think outside the boundaries of monolithic thoughts. That's exactly what he did when he approached me about writing the foreword to his youth book. Arnold's vision is very typical in that he seeks those who have a common ground to traverse the difficult terrain of race and culture through faith and heritage. However, he goes about it in his usual awkward and twisted approach of writing that is often stimulating and provocative to say the least. Taking stories in history that flip traditional views upside down, he draws from a rich well of diversity that pulls pieces of fabric from every part of his being in order that others may have a deeper understanding of themselves, history and God's story. The unlikely twist of someone like myself writing a foreword for his youth book speaks to the complexity of the man and the issues that he brings to the table, whether you like them or not. Black Confederate heritage is not a natural attraction to my Civil Rights era but that's the dichotomy of thought that Arnold elevates in his writings for God's glory. The more I've gotten to know Arnold peeking through his bright veil of Confederate Heritage, the more I am able to see his story as one that would cause America to pause and consider the implications of education reform, a cause that's dear to my own heart.

Arnold is a man, by all accounts, who shouldn't have graduated from college any more than you would expect him to celebrate deep Confederate roots as a Black man in America. It's ironic that the school that I integrated in 1962, The University of Mississippi, would graduate him with honors in 1991. What's even more ironic is that the Journey he experienced educationally is now the Journey that I promote through the Meredith Institute. Being Black and a product of a public school system in Mississippi often doesn't afford escape from poverty, brokenness and despair. But despite the odds, the outcome for Arnold is the reason I chose to walk a lonely road twenty-five years before him and open doors that would greet him with open arms. Arnold doesn't claim success despite a public education, he points to his public education as the backbone that girded him over and through rough waters. Furthermore, it wasn't the rigor of the academics and the emphasis on standardized testing that drove him through this journey, though academics were high on his priority. It was much more. It was his teachers and other tangible things that only reform can bring back to our schools. It was quality learning that propelled the likes of him and others in his era to defeat the odds.

The fourth principle of my Education Bill of Rights is "Quality Learning." It involves a nation where educators and officials collaborate to identify the best evidence-based practices; a nation that rigorously tests classroom products and reforms before spending billions of dollars of taxpayer funds on them, including testing them with smaller class sizes and more experienced teachers; a nation that that does not spend billions of taxpayer dollars on excessive, unreliable and low-quality standardized tests that displace and damage authentic learning; and an education with an absolute minimum of standard-ized tests and a maximum of high-quality, teacher-designed evaluations of student learning and progress. In talking to Arnold, I discovered he took the ACT three times before college. He wasn't proud to tell me his score because it didn't match his academic achieve-ment. Each time, he scored a disappointing thirteen composite score. I asked him how he made it through this. He told me that his teachers never gave up on him. He thought he could conquer the world. He went on to college with the goal of being a Physical

Therapist and the first professor he talked with about his career choice told him that his ACT score was too low to pursue a career in Physical Therapy. At that point, he said he had to rely upon the encouragement of former middle and high school teachers and coaches who taught him to dream big in order to overcome hurdles.

In 1988, Arnold was summoned by a panel of Mississippi State educators at Jackson State University who were studying the reliability of the ACT as a predictor of success in College. What they saw wasn't adding up and they didn't understand as they questioned him about his thoughts on education, success and the relevance of the ACT, which he dis-counted as an indicator as to how he would perform educationally in the future. Nevertheless, Arnold still had to match his ACT score with his academic performance in order to get into Physical Therapy School. Once again, I asked him how he overcame this challenge. He took the test for a fourth time, while a sophomore in college, needing to score a nineteen to qualify for admission. On the day of the test, he completed it within fifteen minutes by marking the third answer choice on his answer sheet. He scored the highest he had ever scored, a nineteen. He went on to graduate with honors from the University of Mississippi School of Physical Therapy in 1991. Arnold is living proof that my initiative to reduce the emphasis on standardized tests is needed. The Billions of dollars spent here could be used in other ways that are more productive toward quality learning. Moreover, many dreams are deferred because of the demand of certain standardized tests.

I believe Arnold was also a benefactor of another aspect of my proposed Bill of Education, "Effective Teachers." Effective teachers are evaluated through fair and aggressive professional peer review, not unreliable standardized test data; and a school where under- performing teachers are coached, mentored and supported, and when necessary fired, through a process of professional review and transparent, timely due process. Moreover, my initiative calls for "Safety, Freedom and Challenge." All three were included in Arnold's experience. A school and a classroom that are safe, comfortable, exciting, happy and well-disciplined; with regular quiet time and play time in the early grades; regular breaks through the school day; daily physical education and recess periods; a healthy, developmentally-appropriate and evidence-based after-school workload; and an atmosphere of low chronic stress and high productive challenge, where children are free to be children as they learn, and children are free to fail in the pursuit of success. Arnold describes the playfulness and yet well-disciplined approach to his early school environment. It is obvious that "Respect for Children and Teachers", another of my proposed measures was an intricate part of Arnold's education. He has a lasting and deep respect for all of his teachers and to a fault points to their love and dedication to him and his peers. These teachers were Arnold's heroes. A nation that respects teachers as well as it respects other elite professions; and considers every child's physical, mental and emotional health, happiness and well-being as critical factors for school behavior, academic achievement and national progress is the nation that will rise to the top.

Finally, I call for a 21st Century education. This is an education with a school and a nation where children and teachers are supported, cherished and challenged, and where teachers are left alone to the maximum extent possible by politicians and bureaucrats to do their jobs – which is to prepare children for life, citizenship, and careers with true 21st century skills: not by drilling them for standardized tests or forcing a culture of stress, overwork and fear upon them, but by helping them fall in love with authentic learning for the rest of their lives, inspiring them with joy, fun, passion, diligence, critical thinking and collaboration, new discoveries and excitement, and having the highest academic expectations of them. When I consider Arnold's story, he received this kind of education. He took full advantage of his opportunities. Sometimes, the things that we had in the past that didn't look so attractive at the time, turn out to be just what we need in life for our future. I'm honored to share in this writing with Arnold. From one brother to another and from Jackson State University to The University of Mississippi, the mission and my struggles were not in vain.

James Meredith, Author

A Mission From God: A Memoir and Challenge for

America

Al Arnold is a descendent of a slave, Turner Hall, Jr. "Uncle Turner," as he was known in his later years, served in the Confederate army as a body servant for two Confederate soldiers and an orderly for Robert E. Lee. As a slave, Turner Hall, Jr. was owned by another prominent Civil War general, Nathan Bedford Forrest.

Al began researching his ancestor's life in 2008. At a family reunion, he saw a newspaper caption indicating his ancestor, Turner Hall, Jr. served Robert E. Lee as an orderly in the Civil War. To Al's amazement, his research found a proud Black Confederate who held both Civil War generals in high esteem, even well after the war. At the age of ninety-five, Turner Hall, Jr. cherished a gift from Nathan Bedford Forrest as one of his most treasured possessions.

Al was further intrigued that his great-great-grandfather was a celebrated man in his community of Hugo, Oklahoma. Blacks and Whites commemorated him as Hugo's "most distinguished citizen" as a result of his Civil War service. Turner Hall, Jr. lived to be a hundred and four years old. He attended the last Civil War reunion in 1938 at Gettysburg, Pennsylvania. Newsreel cameramen captured him displaying his reunion medals as an example of the typical Black Confederate.

In 1940, he was interviewed as a Black Confederate by a nationwide talk radio show in New York City. Turner Hall, Jr. left a trail for his family that Al has uncovered. Al shares his personal journey into his Confederate heritage as a modern Black man. He makes a connection through the life of his ancestor and embraces the premises that history should unite us instead of divide us. He argues that African Americans dishonor their ancestors by attempting to destroy Confederate heritage and by neglecting the historical impact that slaves had on both sides of the Civil War. These are the honest thoughts of a modern Black man who has wrestled with his Confederate heritage while being a Black Christian man in America and who is connected to two famous Civil War generals.

Dedication

To the Administrators, teachers, coaches, staff, cafeteria workers and janitors of Verona Junior High Cardinals and Shannon High School Red Raiders:

And to my all-time favorite cafeteria worker (Gulfport Public Schools) and Mother-in-law, Elnora Posey. (July 2, 1945-October 3, 2012)

It is because of you that we become who we are in the world. Your love, dedication and sacrifice will never be forgotten. You live in the hearts and minds of your students all of our lives. Thank you for caring, sharing and demonstrating faithfulness to your work on our behalf. Moreover, know that you exercised grace and good judgments in your duties and demonstrated a genuine concern for all of your students. Thank you! It is not said enough. Thank you for giving of yourself that we were able to become beacon lights of your labor and demonstrate our oneness and gifts to the world. Forever remembered and not forgotten, you are our heroes.

Preface

A changed man, Indeed! Ten years after the discovery of my Confederate ancestor and twenty-four months after my first book on my heritage and my life is forever altered. It's not so much that my core values have changed. The reason is primarily due to the extended family that I now embrace in the land of the South, my Confederate brothers and sisters. I must admit, that going into this, I was more concerned about what and who I would lose than what I would gain. It can never be popular to write about something that is so unpopular. A Black Man's Confederate Journey is one of those stories that is riddled with snares and glares that would cause the strongest soul to shrink into a cloud of fear. Fortunately, I wasn't given a spirit of fear. Yet, I did not see clearly what I would gain. The gain has been far more valuable and eternal than any loss. To gain a friend is to have one that is closer than a brother. I have gained many. To embrace others who are different than you is far more enriching than to stay on an island of familiarity all of your life. I took a plunge into an unknown territory and found myself at home the farther I got away. I am grateful for finding information on my slave ancestor.

His light has been a path of one amazing discovery after another and has enriched my life beyond measure. Because of him, I have gone to places that I would have never dreamed of going. I have lived more because of his living. He has given me gifts that will remain unredeemable in my days. He has filled my heart with hope that is unquenchable for life.

Black history is unique in that our story involves a people that has demonstrated resilience like none other. We are a peculiar people with stories that have been untold, unknown and hidden from history and the books. These precious jewels are like rare diamonds. Once discovered, because of the oddities and varied circumstances that always surrounds the details of the travail, they give us a sense of mystic that pierces the souls of man in ways that are majestic. A Black Confederate story is one of those mystical travails that is worthy of uncovering. These stories add to the richness of our history and to the peculiarity and diversity of our people. For a modern Black man, the very thought of a Black Confederate can be repulsive. Proudly, as a result of embracing this dilemma through the eyes of my great-great-grand-father, this journey has brought me to a deeper appreciation of who I am as an African American. It has heightened my love for history and the unique roles that African Americans played throughout the development of this great country. I am hopeful that African Americans will learn to embrace the vital era of the Civil War. I continue to believe that embracing our history, instead of rejecting it, will be the bridge that allows our society and communities to heal and grow. I'm thankful that I have had this wonderful growing experience. I extend this writing to the youth of America that they may know the power of alternative thought and the danger of uncritical thinking. To think too critical of oneself can be paralyzing. To think too critical of others is small. However, to think critical of ideas, perceptions and history leads to creativity, freedom and convictions that not only changes your heart but also changes the hearts and minds of those around you for the good of humanity.

Nelson Mandela and Meaningful Contact

To my beloved brothers and sisters who inherited the thorns, thistles, guilt, fruit, shame and spirit of the 60's, we are to never dishonor our ancestors. Our ancestors are the ones whom we are indebted for our liberties.

Moreover, because of these liberties we should seek to honor them by demonstrating the character, dignity, respect and honor that is worthy of their struggles and sacrifices. Can you imagine a day in time when their sacrifices would be discounted as nothing because of the rhetoric of the day or the senseless acts of a few? Perhaps the type of love I am engaging in, through this writing, has never been called upon from our generation, Black or White. Yet, there was one who showed us a more excellent example in this path. He was a man for our generation and a display of God's Grace for the world to see.

When I think of Nelson Mandela, I'm reminded of the scripture that says, "For he who chooses to save his life will lose it and he who chooses to lose his life will save it."

Now here is a man for the ages indeed!

Mandela inspires me to keep loving people who are not like me and to keep running against the wind. He was in-prisoned from 1962-1990. This is why I call him a man of our generation. From our birth until our early adulthood, he languished in a prison cell for freedom. I remember the day he was released from prison as an inspiration that carries me to this day. A mythical figure of a man that I had only heard about from a distance. A fighter, a warrior, a scholar, an activist and giant who was known to be as fierce as a tiger and as wise as a prophet. During his triumphal exit from prison in February of 1990, I couldn't remove the thought from my mind that this man had been a prisoner longer than I had lived on earth. His proclamation was even more amazing. A proclamation of peace and reconciliation toward his White South African brothers as a means to destroy the violence of apartheid as well as the anger and bitterness that so easily beset others. The warfare wasn't over but the weapons of his artillery had changed drastically. The means of seeing the struggle to an end would forever be altered as Mandela relinquished the most powerful deadly foe against his enemies, forgiveness.

He said, "As I walked out the door toward the gate that would lead to my freedom, I knew if I didn't leave my bitterness and hatred behind, I'd still be in prison." He gained his freedom while in- prisoned, not after he was set free. But he exercised his freedom the moment he was unchained. This is quite remarkable if you put yourself in his shoes and ask yourself, what path would you had taken? Apostle Paul understood this when he said, "For though I am free from all, I have made myself a servant to all, that I may win more of them." Mandela, by the unforeseen consequences of having his life taken away, had now gained a freedom that surpassed understanding. Paul, a free man became a slave and Mandela an enslaved man became free. How is this even imaginable?

How could a man after twenty seven years of being a prisoner, forgive so readily, so thorough and so complete? There was no national confession from the oppressor seeking his forgiveness. Yet, through this act of forgiveness, he gave freedom to win others toward reconciliation in a way that shocked our world. His forgiveness was so powerful that it shattered the hatred and bitterness of the oppressor and the oppressed as South Africa became a beacon of light and a glimpse of the reality of what happens when the power of forgiveness is released unconditionally from the heart. The ability to see beyond and into a deeper appreciation of who you are, who others are and how we all stand before a righteous judge as sinners, helps to remove barriers by overcoming the alienation that brokers hostilities and prevent true brotherhood from existing. This act of Nelson Mandela will forever be etched in history as one of man's greatest deeds toward his people. Yet, the act of Mandela in no way compares to the depths of the kind of forgiveness and Grace that Christ has bestowed upon his Church. If one mortal man is able to convey such Grace that caused the world to pause, how much more are we to understand that which Christ did on the Cross when he said, "Father, forgive them, for they know not what they do."

Our generation is not just a byproduct of the last generation but in many ways, have become inprisoned by it. The generation when race didn't matter, my generation, is often sandwiched between our fathers' past memories of racism, hatred, history and bitterness and a new generation of bitterness, hatred and disrespect for one's neighbors and anyone who is not like us. Here lies our greatest potential gift toward humanity. A gift of love that is not bound by cultural norms, protectionism, politics, protest, power and political correctness. Apostle Paul did not encourage people to destroy their culture or their heritage but what he did do was elevate unconditional love above all things. Without Christ, I think this is impossible. But with Him, all things are possible. I can love everybody not because of them, but in-spite of them. The Apostle to the Gentiles was a Jew among Jews. He became a slave by giving up himself for others and won a freedom that allowed him to interact with all cultures and people of various heritages without condemning, attacking or rejecting them. Politics will not give us this. Protests will not share this grace with us. Political correctness will only fight against this. Power structures seek to manipulate and control through guilt and protectionism that is motivated by fear, a paralyzing force. Instead, we must seek to be champions of forgiveness, grace and respect among races, cultures and history.

I believe this is more prone to occur when meaningful contact is made with people of opposing views, cultures and heritages. It is often the opposing views that keep us alienated from one another. This alienation has only been heightened amid divisive hypersensitive environments of social media, political discourse and a computerized age of distance and non-meaningful contact.

"Jesus understood the impact of meaningful contact all too well. He met with the women at the well; an unlikely meeting between a Jew and a Samaritan, not to mention a women. His disciples were astonished by this as their usual travel would have taken them around the city. But not the Master teacher. He said, "I must go through Samaria." He knew everything about this women. He knew things about her that they didn't know. Yet, he drank with her and gave her relief of a thirst that had been unquenchable.

He did it again when he told Zacchaeus, "Come down from that tree, I must go home with you today." Listen to his Words. He evokes the same kind of urgency as with the women at the well when He said, "I must." Zacchaeus, a Roman tax collector, was considered a sinner by Jews. His collections would have been used for a secular government system and for the support of pagan gods. Yet, Jesus initiated contact with him, changing his life. This meaningful contact works both ways. As long as it's meaningful, the potential for reconciliation is beyond measure. What do I mean by meaningful contact? I mean in and through Christ you are willing to forbear different cultures and heritages with His heart, eyes, ears, tongue, hands and feet. Not yours, but His. As a result, nothing will stop you from loving, seeking and experiencing life with the other group. The women who had a blood disease understood this kind of contact. Her only thought was, "If I could just touch him." And she did! Her heart, eyes, ears, mind and body was focused on Him. In the noise of the day, with all of the distractions, she understood one essential thing. All that matters is that I make contact with Him. Other examples of meaningful contact by the Master teacher is when he takes spit and mud to touch the blind man's eyes so that he could see. He used spit again to heal a man who was deaf by putting his fingers in his ears and touching his tongue. Again, he was hanging out at the home of a Pharisee when a sinner women washed his feet. His host thought for certain that this man could not possible know that the lady washing his feet was a sinner. He was never afraid to move toward people with whom he was socially not suppose to have contact. Yet, when he made contact or when people made contact with Him, peoples' lives changed. Entire communities and households changed. It's this meaningful contact through His grace that we need today. Nothing breaks down barriers like this kind of contact.

Apostle Paul understood this, as well. In one instance he said, "I am obligated to the Greek and to the barbarian." Greeks considered everyone who was not Greek as a barbarian. Paul said, "I love them, too." Then he would say, "To the Jew, I became like a Jew." Why would Paul say I became a Jew when he was a Jew among Jews? Because Paul understood the need for meaningful contact. He knew the importance of being all things to all kinds of people that he may win some for Christ. He was free to go in and out of different cultures and heritages for the sake of the Gospel. Oh, that Christians would do this today! Too few are willing to live out the Gospel in this way. This kind of Gospel living, is radical, overcomes fears and sets captives free. It doesn't call for anyone to forgo their culture or heritage. No, it causes you to go into their culture or heritage with love. Meaningful contact is a Christ-like heart, mind, eyes, ears and body directed toward people who are very different than you.

One of Mandela's prison guards was young, energetic and very pro-apartheid when he first met Mandela. They developed a relationship that tore down their barriers. Meaningful contact makes a difference that protest, politics, protectionism, power, and political correctness will never be able to achieve. These two men developed forgiveness, Grace and respect for each other. That guard, Christi Brand said, "So many things have changed. I still work on the island but now I work with the same people who once were prisoners. And we are all free. We are all equal. It is better for all of us."

(Andrew Meldrum, Cape Town Saturday 19 May 2007 21.18 EDT The Guardian). Here is my freedom to live, embrace, enjoy, rejoice, share, cultivate, mourn and unite with my brothers and sisters throughout the South. To God be the glory!

Acknowledgments

I want to thank my dad, Tommie Arnold, and his siblings, Uncle Eugene (Emma Jean), Willie (Pat), Earnest (Mary Nell), Herbert (Currie), Davis, Ralph (Priscilla), aunt Pearl (Willie), Avis (Aldophus); and my deceased uncles, Emmitt and Leroy (not forgotten). Every year for the past seventeen years, they have hosted our family reunion. Family has been the main focus of our gatherings and their efforts. They have shown the next generation how to serve, love, and forgive. They did not hide the claims of their great-grandfather. Nor have they ever hidden any birth claims in the family. They celebrated his history in the Civil War and our history as his descendants. In doing this, they have afforded the entire family and me a richer understanding of our ancestor and who he was as a person. This has brought us to a better under-standing of who we are as a family. Thanks to Aunt Pearl, our Senior Family Historian. Her assistance and previous years of work on our family history made this possible.

The spark of this work was greatly enhanced and stimulated as a result of the research, support, and findings through the Oklahoma Historical Society. I cannot thank their staff enough for the wonderful assistance they have provided in this development. As with the first book, I am grateful for the work of Dianne Thornton of Crescent City Music Services for her work on the cover design. Your talents are exceptional. It was a sure joy to work with artist and fellow Black New Yorker and Southerner at heart, Gregory Newson, for his illustrations.

I would also like to thank all of the supporters of my first book. To the three thousand and more readers, I want to thank you for believing in the South, the commitment to history and allowing me to have my say in a world that often doesn't want to hear anything different than what one believes in. The support and encouragement has been overwhelming. I have travelled to over seven states and spoken at many venues to some of the best people in the South. The food, fun, stories, laughter and fellowship has been some of the sweetest frames of hospitality that I have witnessed in my short lifetime.

I would like to thank my wife and kids who continue to show the bravest trust in me, by standing by me, in this Confederate journey. Your strength and willingness to loan me out to this cause is another testimony to the power of love, the importance of family and the Grace of God. You continue to tolerate my zeal for history, the Civil War and Pappa Turner. Your support means the world to me.

Finally, to the youth that I have met during this journey, thank you. I have been overjoyed to share this story with you in person. It is because of you that I have decided to present this version of the story. I was young when I fell in love with history. Many times, when I travelled over the last two years, I was reminded of the hope that I had when I was just a youth by looking into your eyes. It is a pure hope that is not defined by the boundaries that society holds you too. To think critically, to dream big and to live dynamically is the hope that is offered to you in this writing. May you take history and absorb the richness of it and live today knowing that your paths have been laid out before the foundations of this world by a Great Creator and through the means of men and women who came before you at His discretion. Honor Him and honor them and you will live well brave ones.

Growing Up Southern

"There was an old man, his name was Uncle Ned, he died long– long– ago. He had no hair on the top of his head, the place where the wool ought to grow.

"Lay down the shovel and the hoe, pick up the fiddle and the bow, there's no more work for poor Uncle Ned, he is gone where the good darkies go, he is gone where the good darkies go. (Chorus)

"His fangers was long, like the cane in da break, he had no eyes to see. He had no teeth to eat the hoe cake, so he had to let the hoe cake be." (Chorus)

This is a slave song handed down to my family by my maternal grandmother. Growing up, my family loved to sing the lyrics of "Uncle Ned."

This song was my only direct lens into the eyes of a slave. It was about a man, "Uncle Ned." I pictured Uncle Ned as a strong-framed man with a worn-out body due to hard labor. He was full of wisdom and highly regarded. He was a man strong in stature. A man that was so vital to his community, a song was put to words to remember him. His meals were meager but satisfying. His eyes were dim and he had very strong hands that could grip a knot in a young boy. He was a good man.

Slaves were musically inclined and celebrations were woven into their social structure. Slaves longed to be free and heaven was certainly an option. Indeed, heaven was their freedom. I've often wondered if singing about that fiddle, at such a young age, is the reason that bluegrass is my favorite music. After I discovered the banjo hails from the continent of Africa, I realized that I had every right to bluegrass than any hillbilly in Kentucky. It was just in my bones. None of the slave narratives in school made me feel good about slavery. Uncle Ned gave me a different glimpse. It didn't take away the gore of slavery but it did give me a different perspective. It was a perspective of hope. Yet, Uncle Ned was a fictional character. Or, was he? I wasn't sure. He was a slave in a song.

Years later I would learn of another slave named Uncle Turner. The only difference was that this uncle was not a fictional character in a song. He was my great-great-grandfather. This discovery would begin my journey into my Confederate heritage.

It was at a family reunion in 2008 when my Aunt Pearl revealed our family heritage book. In that book was a photo that I had seen many times. But there was something else that struck me as remarkably odd. There was a caption from a newspaper article, "Turner Hall, A Real Pioneer" that read, "he was an orderly for Robert E. Lee."

As a young African American boy growing up in northeast Mississippi, history was always a favorite subject during my formative years. Having a photographic memory, I devoured essay questions on American and Mississippi history exams. History surrounding wars were especially interesting to me. I marveled at historical figures and embraced stories of personal triumph and heroism. The one figure that I regretted, as a very young historian, was Benedict Arnold. The fact that he was a known traitor during the American Revolution and carried my last name gave me chills. I was fearful that one day I would come to learn that he was my ancestor.

Ancestry has always been intriguing to me. What human being doesn't want to know where they come from? I believe I am not alone in this quest. If the truth were told, many African Americans want to know more about their ancestors. However, records are so vague in our history. Records only go so far due to historical issues of how slaves were considered property and not people. It's only so far that we can go back and then we hit that inevitable wall of slavery that we all know is there. So, many just never muster up the energy to start. As much as I would love to go further than I have, I find a bit of relief that I will never be able to trace a connection of my name to the most familiar traitor in American history: Benedict Arnold. So, in a sense, I am protected. Shielded from the shame. Indeed, the shame of it all is enough to stop the most resourceful person in their pursuit of their own personal ancestry.

Yet, as a young boy, nothing intrigued me more than personal family history. I was raised during a time when bravery was inspirational and heroism was awarded at great sacrifice. My mother's family consisted of a matriarch and eight daughters. My father's family consisted of a patriarch, matriarch, nine boys, and two girls. There are countless cousins and extended family members that came from these family trees. During those years, photos were a tangible way for most families to keep record. There was no better way in my family to review our history than to ask my grandmother to show the family portraits. She kept them in a cedar chest in her home. It would be years later that we would learn the value of cedar wood. The house burned, destroying all of her possessions except those priceless photos preserved by the cedar. It was in those photos that I first saw a picture of my great-great-grandfather,

Turner Hall, Jr., the inspiration of this book. I didn't know his name at the time and not much was said about him. I remember him being a grand figure of a man. He was tall, handsome, and had a pleasant disposition, unlike the many faces of the old photos of his day. I remember him standing proudly with an alarmingly huge hat and a dazzling blue jacket with large buttons on each side. He stood with a large frame in front of what appeared to be a row of very small white homes. My grandmother would say, "That's my Pappa." This photo, I later learned was her mother's father and my great-great-grandfather, Turner Hall, Jr.

Time and time again we would sit on the floor and she would pull out photos and allow us to look and ask questions. We usually didn't touch the photos. These photos demanded respect and the best behavior. At the time, we didn't know where she kept the photos. She would always make us stay in the front room as she retrieved the photos from the cedar chest. Another great family photo of superb importance and personality to the family was of my grandfather's father, Lucian "Paw Dick" Arnold. This photo, like that of Turner Hall, Jr., is etched in the memory of all the Arnold clan. In the photo, "Paw Dick" is sitting in a chair with his wooden peg leg and a huge cigar in his mouth—exuding nothing but pride, sincerity, and character. An annual review and conversation of these two photos and many more was like a ritual for elders in the family and a rite of passage for all youngsters. The fruits and labor of these two men would define who we were and who we would aspire to be as individuals of this family. Their pictures portrayed self-esteem, hard work, honesty, faithfulness, forwardness, faith, perseverance, hope, and integrity. Their kids would be beacon lights into the eyes and hearts for the next two generations of Arnolds. A thread of family loyalty and history was established around these photos and family gatherings that continue to this day. The Annual family reunion at the home front in Monroe County, Mississippi, is much like a yearly community celebration.

You know you are getting off to a great Southern start in life when your dad gives you a five dollar bill and tells you to give your brother half of it and all you know to do is to rip ole Abe half in two and hand one part of his face to your brother and keep the other for yourself. That's exactly what my sister did when instructed to share this five dollar bill. Black youth, especially in Mississippi, are often portrayed as a half split five dollar bill. There is a half face on each side telling very different stories of Blacks and Whites. I am blessed to say that this divide is not the experience of my Southern rearing. As much as this five dollar bill was one piece of money, my Southern childhood was one big piece of divided joy. We taped that five dollars back together and it was as good as gold at the local store.

Just as I didn't initially appreciate that one half of Abe's face wasn't worth a dime without the other half, I came to understand that one half of Mississippi wasn't good without the other. In fact, my Southern experience was rooted in this concept primarily through an integrated school environment. I moved from a school in Monroe County to Lee County during the second grade. With the last name Arnold, the alphabetical order put me behind a white girl name Laura Anglin. For the next ten years, Laura and I would sit next to each other and forged our halves of a community together. But we were not the only ones; these dynamic relationships played out throughout our schools. We represent a race-less generation that is often forgotten about. I call it the generation when race didn't matter. Every generation has its defining marks to signify the error that they grew up. Generation X ranges from 1961-1981, Generation Y ranges from early 1980's to early 1990's and the Millenniums typically range from the mid 1990's to the early 2,000's. There is overlap in these generations. For the most part, you can measure some of the issues of importance of the respective generations based upon these date ranges. I was born in 1968, which places my generation as X. In fact, I would say the latter part of that generation. There was something special about that generation that separated us from the muck and miry clay of racism. I now realize that a big part of the glue that kept us together was our teachers.

The impact that teachers have on their students is life-long. We had teachers who made a real impact on a generation. Not only did they guide us away from racism and bigotry in the heartland of Mississippi, they lived by example and showed us the way. It is because of them, that we were the generation when race didn't matter in Mississippi. When I was in grade school, it is clear to say that I was an unruly child. Plagued with the brains of a potential academic scholar and yet with all the makings of a class clown. I was as unpredictable as a polecat. Had it not been for the mindful eye of two of the grandest White men I had ever seen, perhaps my foolishness would have overcome my youthfulness and rendered me another statistic. Mr. Robert Long and Mr. John Kitchens were giants during my middle school years. Mr. Kitchens reminded you of a stern, rough riding biker kind of guy that exuded authority like none other. Mr. Long wore cowboy boots and stood at least 6'3" in my eyes. These were real men teaching elementary school. Not only were they giants in our lives, they carried giant boards with them to enforce their authority. What would often look like rowing oars for a championship boat race were regular instruments of discipline that ensured the elementary hallway stayed free of debris. That's right, the ol' paddling board. I'm sad to say that I had to touch my toes far too many times but not with these men. You did everything in your power to muster a "yes, sir" and a "no, sir whenever they asked you a question. The surprise for many of us was to discover these men exercising grace and mercy as much as they did exact righteous punishment for our misdeeds. They were known for competing with each other in the course of a day. Looking back, one of their joys had to be the sure fun of terrifying the students. It worked. They would catch us in our normal mischievous deeds and call us into the hallway only to swing their paddles at the back of their shoes three or four times as hard as they could. The boards would sound so loud against their shoes that the poor souls left in the class rooms were horrified. In order to carry out their hoax, we had to play our part upon return to the room, lest the punishment indeed fit the crime. After the classroom bell would ring, you would still smell the smoke from the shoes in the hallway and that was enough to keep everyone on an even keel, at least until the next day.

There is no forgetting Mr. Johnny Bell, a middle grade math teacher with a great love for kids. He was loved and respected by all. Can you imagine? All of the kids loving a math teacher? He was that kind of guy. He ranked really high with the board, as well. You didn't want him to call you to the hallway. There was Mrs. Shirley, our English teacher; not a kinder and more merciful soul I can give to you in this writing than this dear one. She endured children for generations and I am daily indebted to her grace. My actions in her class would bar any kid today from ever entering a school again.

We simply didn't know how caring their care for us really was. We live in a punitive educational system today, and for some reason, the punishments don't work. We were punished with love, tenderness and a few swats on your behind if you got out of order. That combination made it all come together in the end.

There were two more prominent men who appeared in my life as I entered Junior High School. If Mr. Long and Mr. Kitchens were competing for smoke at the grand barbecue of discipline, we now enter the Grand National Championship of champions. Mr. Lynn Payne and Mr. Bobby Ray Patterson were two of the strongest Black men that I had ever seen. It wasn't smoke that we could smell in the hallway after a whipping from one of these men, it was the flames still burning that calmed the entire school. Imagine Smoking Joe Frazier and The Rock telling you to pull your pants up and sit down. There was no questioning and no disrespect. It was "Yes, sir, how high do you want them, sir?" None of that Black and White stuff that you often see spewing from the mouths and hearts of parents today when their kids are disciplined to the slightest degree. There wasn't a claim of unfairness. In my own estimation, I crossed the line deserving of being expelled at least on two occasions. Thankfully, I never got expelled. It was certainly God's Grace. A grace that was in the hearts of all of the teachers, coaches, staff members and administrators. Looking back at these men and women, I am able to evaluate their tenderness, mercy and service to our common growth. Never was there a time that I can remember that a parent had to come to the school. They were an extension of our parents. In fact, had my mother been called for any reason, I was guaranteed another whipping, as was the case with my classmates. At our school, we knew who the bosses were and though we tried them in every way, they never stopped loving, never stopped disciplining and never stopped caring for us.

Let me shed more light on the matter. When I got kicked out of Bible Class for being a class clown, I was taken to Mr. Eddie Cooley's office. Just picture in your mind a tall, white man who had a gentle voice and looked like the best granddaddy in the world. Or picture the Deacon in the church that everybody loved and everybody knows is an upright man. Well, this was our principal. Instead of sending me home, what does he do? He tells me to come to his office to have Bible class with him each day. This grace was so pervasive that there was simply no way out of it. Wow! How do you escape this kind of grace? We had no-where to run or fall but into the loving arms of a gracious God through our teachers. Unfortunately, teachers, staff members, administrators and coaches are not told until it's too late 'your words or your actions were a principle means that saved me.' In reality, this is what is being played out in the classroom every day. The very reason I love libraries today is not because I loved the library when I was a child. It wasn't because I loved to read. No, I loved the librarian, Mrs. Anne Radojcsics. I could never understand why she was always so kind. I carried on mischief every day and almost at every opportunity in that library of hers. When one of my teachers would throw me out of a classroom into the hallway, she would come by and pinch me on the cheeks and say, "You are out here again, Al?" But that wasn't all she would do. She would drop a book in my lap and hurry away to the next student.

The old saying, "Sticks and stones may break my bones but words do not hurt me," is one of deception. Words do hurt. I remember once being hurt by words from an opposing football player after a Tuesday night football game. I was in the 8th grade and had played a cross town rival when, at the end of the game, one of their players jumped on our bus and said some insulting things about our head football coach, James Sprayberry. Our coaches were also our heroes. Hands down, these were the men and women who shaped our thoughts and molded our character. I got so upset that I ran after the guy and picked up a log from a burning fire and threw it at the kid just as he entered his locker room. One problem, I forgot to take off my jersey. I was readily identified to my coaching staff as the kid who threw the burning log into the locker room. Deservedly, I was released from the football team the next day. Coach Sprayberry, sometime later, found out the details of what happened. He extended me grace to re-join the team after giving me rebuke and encouragement over the matter.

Words can help, too. My life has shown me this over and over again. They are masterfully helpful when used appropriately. One of the most helpful set of words that has ever come to me were words unexpected. They found me at a critical time in my life. It was during my transition from junior high to high school. The assistant principal of the school, Mr. Lemois Oswalt, was also the bus driver for our neighborhood. He was tough yet gentle in his demeanor. A respectful man who played his role in our discipline very well. I will never forget this day as long as I live. It was the last bus drop for me as a 9th grader living on John F. Kennedy Drive. The next bus that stopped in front of that house would be the following fall high school term. He stopped me as I exited the bus. As I turned around, he looked me straight in the eye and said, "Al, you can do it."

These were the first words of affirmation that I had ever heard in my life that stuck with me. This was a white man speaking to me in a way that had never before registered in my mind. He was saying, "Despite your behavior Al, you can do it!" At that moment, I felt something inspiring. One thing for sure, I knew that Grace had been shared with me in an abundant way. My tenure at this school wasn't deserving of this encouragement and affirmation. Countless times, I had been to that office; so many times that I had my own special seat where they would allow me to sit and pull it all together before returning to class. How could these words be coming out if his mouth?

High school was an extension of the same grace. We were wrapped in hearts of love, devotion, sacrifice and grace by all of our coaches, administrators and teachers. There was less need for discipline in High School because the groundwork had been done in the previous years. My hero, Coach Lee Gardner, was one of such character. I remember his brute strength, straight forwardness and gentleness as the kind of man I would one day want to be. Once, a pair of football cleats came up missing from the locker room. It was only one pair out of a hundred, but it mattered to him that honesty and integrity was instilled in the team. He called everyone together and gave a speech to the effect that "I expect them to be back in my office the next day." The next day, they were returned. The poor soul who took those cleats was probably pranking another kid but the prank was on him. Once that man spoke, you acted out of respect for who he was.

My favorite high school teacher, Sandra Rogers, was in no way short on Grace. By this time, I still hadn't worked out all of my kinks and remember throwing a smoke bomb through her cracked window, which landed under her desk. It filled the room with smoke and caused an evacuation of her class. I was as guilty as a Baptist boy sitting on the mourning bench waiting to be baptized. The only other person who knew it was her. And then there was the mastery of mischief by my co-conspirator, Joe Mask and me. Joe, a tall lanky White guy brought the cigarette and I brought the large pack of "firecrackers", as we say in Mississippi. We staged a bathroom ruckus that will never be forgotten. The plan was set. The target was the main bathroom right across from the principal's office. We both were granted bathroom passage as planned. We removed the butt of the cigarette and placed the stem of the fireworks into one end of the cigarette. Placing this contraption above the toilet stall and out of sight, the trap was set. Joe had assured me that a cigarette, once lit, would not go out until it burns to the opposite end. We casually strolled back to Mr. Gregory's math class separately and settled in for the big dance. Ten minutes later and the greatest mischief of my school career was in the record book.

This one, however, was only a close second to an act that occurred during middle school. It was that Bible class again. I hated that class. I decided one morning to delay the class by causing the bell in the building to go silent. Once again, bathroom privileges weren't always for relieving myself. Mostly, it was to relieve myself from the constant mischief that ran in my head daily. After finding the wires to the bell and cutting them with the scissors that I retrieved off the teacher's desk, I returned from my bathroom break. By cutting this wire, the entire building was rendered

15

without a school bell. It must have been an hour before anyone realized that we had failed to exchange classes. There I sat, steeped in my sin of mischief at the highest level and as proud as a peacock. It was just another great day at my school where grace and mischief ran counter to each other every day. Grace prevailed!

What could rescue a soul such as this? Only the Grace of God shared by many teachers, administrators and coaches who faithfully discharged their duties to us daily. Their words, their hugs and their patience can never be forgotten. Imagine, if you can when there was a time when Black Kids and White kids went to school every day on the same buses where White teachers and Black teachers were all entrusted to be their parents away from home. I know. It's hard to imagine, but it happened for a period in Mississippi. On graduation day, the first tear rolled out of my eye when I laid my eyes on my friend, Laura. She and I cried as we realized how woven our spirits had become. We served in student council together. We were the ones to put up the American Flag every morning with the greatest respect for that duty and our country's Flag. We learned to type together with her mother as our teacher, enduring our every act of disobedience. Once I wasn't feeling too well and these were her words through a handwritten note, "Al, Smile! God loves you! (And so does everyone else). Your "little-buddy". P.S. Please Smile, Laura. This is the kind of love we were surrounded with. I still have that note today. It was written thirty-one years ago.

When I was a young man, having been firmly established by strong family connections through Christian values, personal responsibility and strong work ethics from both sides of the family, it was time to depart home and pursue a college education. My parents were among the working poor; cut off from opportunities largely due to dropping out of high school. This was the case with many Blacks and Whites in rural Mississippi. Hard work was a viable option in their day and that is what they pursued. They succeeded by the sweat of their brow. My mom worked in a wood factory making doors and my father worked in a meat processing company. Mother, many years later, obtained a GED and went on to graduate from college. My father, without an education, worked his way up to head plant manager and supervised the entire night shift operation at a huge processing plant. He told me once that he never worked a job that he didn't quickly find himself as supervisor. With only a few exceptions, I represented the first generation of family members to leave home to pursue a college degree. I soon realized how privileged I was to have such an opportunity.

At this time in my life, I began to think of the historical implications of the plight of my family and those who had prevailed over many hardships. Furthermore, what was I to make of my forefathers? They knew nothing but hard work. Who were these men and how did they leave such strong family ties? It was also during these years that I first became familiar with the historical aspects of slavery, the Confederacy, and the implication of these issues upon African Americans, the State of Mississippi, the South, and this country. Having chosen an historically Black college and university in Jackson, Mississippi, Jackson State University, I embarked upon areas of learning that offered historical nuances unique to the African American experience. This was a solid start that would prepare me for a life in the South. My high school guidance counselor had warned me that if I attended a black college, I would learn to hate White people. Well, one thing that I did not learn at JSU was to hate white people. However, what I did learn was to think critically of other black folk and to come to the realization that some black folks are just as crazy as some white folks.

I would have one more dose of the power of words coming from the mouth of a teacher. Approaching my third year of college and my first attempt to get into physical therapy school, I was taking some high-level science courses. Dr. Henderson, Ph.D., taught one in particularly, Physiology. She was a strong Black female professor at Jackson State University. I was at a point of crisis in my belief that I could succeed at the task ahead of me, which was to successfully graduate from physical therapy school. One day in lab class, she was having a conversation with a few of us about our future goals. She obviously felt my concerns somehow and these words came out of her mouth, "You can do it." From that day forward, I never once again doubted my abilities. These words had come to me twice at a moment of crisis in my belief. Both times, they came from teachers. Teachers leave inheritances and a great inheritance have I received in Mississippi.

Next was a largely all-white experience at the School of Physical Therapy at The University of Mississippi, just across town from Jackson State. I left JSU and graduated as the only African American male in a class of forty-two graduates in the School of Physical Therapy in 1991. Although there were a few JSU professors and many of my peers who deemed Ole Miss off limits during that time, most professors encouraged students to go to Ole Miss, if accepted, to show that we were capable of competing. I remember the pressure of being the only Black male in my physical therapy class. There were two Black females in my class. It was really tough at one point. I was doing so well in school and actually thought everybody in the school had to think I was cheating. My white peers thought I was a Black genius and had me over for dinner many nights. That served a poor boy like me well during those days. What they didn't know is that I had studied every aspect of anatomy the previous summer months and had memorized every bone, muscle, and nerve in the body; I could name them and recall everything about them with my eyes closed before the first class.

I went on to graduate from Ole Miss with honors. I was voted the most outstanding student by the faculty and received the Minority Scholarship of Academic Excellence for the highest academic GPA of all minority students in America from the American Physical Therapy Association (I was the first African American to receive the award in1990). I can only recall one negative racial experience during my enrollment at the University of Mississippi. It was not among my classmates and surprisingly, at the time, didn't come from my faculty. I had the best support from the faculty while at Ole Miss. I came to realize that many of the stereotypes about going to any of the branches of the University of Ole Miss medical school branches were just stereotypes and perceptions. I found no real reality in the horror that many carried on their shoulders. I soon learned that the primary reason it was so hard to get in was because it was even harder to get out. This was the real issue. When I got into the Physical Therapy program, I learned that the administrators at the school were more concerned about graduating students successfully rather than having an easy open-door policy of admission. Because of this, admission standards were very high and highly competitive.

After college, I moved to New Orleans for six months but soon returned to Mississippi. Kissing the ground, I vowed never to leave her again. From that day to now, I always refer to my beloved state as, "The Great State of Mississippi!" In all of this, here is the thing that I have come to appreciate. I wasn't special. My teachers were special! Oh, how I can see it now. From kindergarten to college, special teachers, administrators and coaches leave an inheritance across this land.

The War that Made a New People

I can't count the times I've used the expression, "You can't choose your family, you're born into it." My mom once told me that only God gets you out of a thing, over a thing, and through a thing without changing a thing. The War Between the States, from the perspective of most African Americans my age, is perfectly summed up in this statement. These are our sentiments of the hundred years after the war. Our people got out of slavery and made it over the next hundred years and suffered throughout the process—but the issue had not changed. The slave received his freedoms with the 13th, 14th, and 15th amendments but did not fully see the fruition of those amendments for another hundred years after the Civil War.

Let's put that in perspective for an African American such as myself. In my research, I discovered that my great-great-grandfather returned to Okolona, Mississippi after the war. The Civil War ended in

1865. I was born in Okolona, Mississippi, in 1968. That's a hundred and three years later. The year I was born was one of the most turbulent times during the civil rights movement for African Americans. It was the year Dr. Martin Luther King, Jr. was killed. I didn't study this era history significantly until I got to college. By the time I became a grown man, I had to develop a perspective and appreciation for those who had struggled during the civil rights movement. I honestly hadn't developed critical thoughts of the war between the states and the times which preceded this era, though the historical connections were later evident to me. I call this gap the hundred year gap.

My questions about the hundred year gap were largely relegated to mystery. I wanted badly to fill this void. It was like the gap between the Old Testament and the New Testament. There is a total disconnect to the Civil War for African Americans in my generation. We learned little, if anything, of the Negro's role in the war. For my generation, slavery represented the Old Testament. The hundred years after the war represents the gap in which God did not speak (between the Old and New Testament). The civil rights movement was our New Testament. It was our beginning. Yet, the actual historical beginning had come a hundred years previously. Out of darkness and confusion God waited four hundred years to set in motion events that would be the making of a people. It was the Civil War. I have come to appreciate that this making of a people was not only for former slaves but for former slave owners, as well. Redemption and freedom would come to both people and forge a nation of greatness.

Therefore, I believe this hundred year gap is a primary cause of disconnect between today's contemporary Negro and the Civil War. I would suspect for Whites my age the same could be said. The only difference is many Whites have recorded historical connections. On the other hand, African Americans my age know nothing about the Civil War because of the hundred-year gap. Whites my age will quickly tell you they had nothing to do with slavery. This is the tension that has existed over the past fifty years for adults my age. In essence, African Americans my age don't want to know about slavery and our White peers don't want to be blamed for slavery. That leaves only two factions to dialogue over the most important war of our country. Those that are trying to hold on to their rightful Confederate heritage and those that were abused during the civil rights era of our country seeking their rightful civil rights as a people. Consequently, these two opposing forces would be the farthest from understanding each other's perspective.

Who doesn't want God on their side? Every man desires to be right in his own eyes today. It was true then and it's true now. Not only did the North and South believe that God was on their side, the slaves fervently believed that God was on their side. Southerners saw their plight just as the early founding fathers of our country saw themselves fighting to be liberated from British rule. It was not a rebellion but a revolution. Thus, just as God had caused a rag-tag militia group of civilians to prevail against the British army, so too would He cause the South to prevail against the tyrannical rule of the Northern government. Abolitionist and radical Northern Republicans saw the South as an immoral aristocracy and claimed God to be defenders of their cause. Abolitionist John Brown said:

> "I am now quite certain that the crimes of this guilty land will never be purged away; but with Blood. I had as I now think vainly flattered myself that without very much bloodshed, it might be done." (John Brown, Charleston, VA Dec. 2nd, 1859)

The Civil War, in my opinion, is the war of all wars for our country. It is this war that is mostly responsible for who we are as a nation. Because of this war, we became a successful nation militarily, socially, and spiritually. Of course, the social advancement was delayed for millions. Military tactics from the Civil War were incorporated in World War I and World War II. Had it not been for the Civil War, Hitler may have very well prevailed. Many of our land grant colleges, including the historical Black Alcorn State University in Lorman, Mississippi, are a result of the legislation immediately following the Civil War. The 13th, 14th, and 15th amendments giving former slaves their freedom, equal rights, and protection of the laws and a right to vote respectively came as a direct result of the Civil War. As an African American, I am compelled to study this war like no other.

Perhaps no other human race has been discredited in the annals of wartime history than the African American. Although, unquestionably, there is no American war that he cannot be found to have participated in and yet his efforts are usually minimized in significance. From the Revolutionary War to the Civil War, there he was, fighting, serving, and dying for a struggle. The struggle for the African American, until this point in modern history, usually involved loyalty, courage, servant-hood, and manhood. As much as I want to believe my ancestor raised an army of slaves, escaped north, and joined the Northern army, that didn't happen. Perhaps these are the hopes of many contemporary African Americans. The hope of many would be to dream of heroism that aligns with their current ideology. However, the Negro slave was much more complex than that. Although, some did have the opportunity to escape on the back of the Union army and through other routes, many never came into proximity of a Union military. For those who were fortunate enough to trail behind a Union regiment, many were abandoned, suffered for lack of food and shelter, and were often sold back into slavery, drowned or killed.

Many slaves would fight with their boyhood masters. At the start of the war, in particularly, there was no promise of freedom attached to the victor of the war. No promises had been granted to the Negro that would have led him to believe if he fought on either side of the conflict that he would be better off. Overwhelmingly, neither the South nor the North employed Black soldiers in the beginning of the war. By the end of the war, both sides either had used Negro soldiers or had passed legislation to incorporate Negro soldiers.

However, that doesn't mean the Negro was doing nothing, as often betrayed by modern African-American thought. He was not standing by watching White folks fight. They were intimately involved in various ways. They served as scouts, spies, cooks, blacksmiths, trench diggers, and a host of other support roles. Some were cavalry men, regular soldiers, and snipers. The Negro was the master forager on either side of the war. In fact, the entire Confederate army was supported by an infrastructure of Black men who served throughout the war. Contrary to what many African Americans believe, Abraham Lincoln did as much as he could to stabilize slavery in the southern states as any Southerner. Moreover, slaves were not welcomed in the North. White Northerners during the war were often more racist than Southerners toward Blacks. Here is a capture of what happened to Blacks in New York City after the fall of Vicksburg and Port Hudson:

"The mob was composed of the lowest and most degraded of the foreign population (mainly Irish), raked from the filthy cellars and dens of the city, steeped in crimes of the deepest dye, and ready for any act, no matter how dark and damnable; together with the worst type of our native criminals, whose long service in prisons of the country, and whose training in the Democratic party, had so demoralized their natures, that they were ever on the hunt for some deed of robbery or murder. Never, in the history of mob-violence, was crime carried to such an extent. Murder, arson, robbery, and cruelty reigned triumphant throughout the city, day and night, for more than a week. Hundreds of the Blacks, driven from their homes, and hunted and chased through the streets, presented themselves at the doors of jails, prisons, and police stations, and begged admission. Thus, did they prowl about the city, committing crime after crime; indeed, in point of cruelty, the Rebellion was transferred from the South to the North." (Wells Brown, *The Negro in The American Rebellion*, Chapter XXVI–1867)

Many of the Union generals had no tolerance for Negros. General Tecumseh Sherman had a strong disdain for the Negro. Any serious student of history knows that Lincoln used the issue of slavery as a prop to lure the Southern states back into the Union. His primary goal was to preserve the Union, not to free the slaves. Had he had his way, the South could have kept their slaves. Lincoln was not a member of the Radical Republicans that promoted the Civil War as an end to slavery. Yet, we don't see this version of Lincoln portrayed in the 2012 movie, Lincoln. We see him as the great deliverer of the slave. African Americans did not hesitate to support this movie nor did they protest Lincoln's Pro-Southern views. Should we remove Abraham Lincoln's portrait from the five-dollar bill? If we follow the logic of some modern African Americans to remove every vestige and symbol of those who supported slavery we would have to destroy the North much as the north destroyed the South during the Civil War. Is that a logical thing to do? Is that an absurd thought? Of course, it is illogical to think this way.

A very high percentage of Mississippi Confederate regiments had Negro servants at the time of their departure. My great-great-grandfather is noted to have "flunked" for two Confederate soldiers. As a result, many young Negros departed with the sons of their master or their master themselves. These same servants would stay by their masters' sides throughout the war. Many would go to great extremes to find the dead bodies of their comrades to ensure that the body was returned home for proper burial.

Has Birthday - Turner Hall

"Uncle Turner Hall has taken the spotlight for being Hugo's most distinguished resident.

The one hundred year old colored man was born October 10th, 1840, a slave on a Mississippi Plantation and was therefore a century old last Friday.

In June of 1938, he was honored by the United States government and given a free trip to the last Civil war veterans reunion at Gettysburg, Virginia and was again honored by appearing on the "We the People" nation-wide radio hock up in New York sponsored by the Sanka Coffee company, in May this year.

Uncle Turner was brought to Hugo from Mississippi many years ago and has resided here ever since. Uncle Turner is a Civil War veteran, having served in the southern army and was orderly for General Robert E. Lee commander of the southern armies and was present when Gen. Lee surrendered to General Grant. His memory is excellent and he enjoys relating his experiences in connection with his services for the famous southern general. His claims to this distinction have been verified from records in the war department." (*Hugo Daily News* October 13, 1940. Oklahoma Historical Society)

My Beloved Mississippi &
The Confederate Flag

Charles Rangel, Democrat Congressman in New York, quickly became a notable Black politician whom I didn't like for his comments; particularly his, "who in the crap wants to live in Mississippi" comment in 2006. At the time of his comment, I was thirty-seven years old. I fired back at the TV and yelled, "Who in God's heaven wants to live in New York, Charlie?" Charlie later apologized and I had to come to grips with what I thought he meant in his famous blasphemy against the hospitality state. I took him not to mean anything derogative toward the people of Mississippi. In fact, he released a statement verifying his intent was not to offend anyone. "I just love New York so much that I can't understand why everyone wouldn't want to live here." My sentiments exactly!

Regarding the great state of Mississippi, we have it all. Good living, fishing, hunting, great food, the best music, and hospitality. I like to say that most of every-thing good in every other state got its start in Mississippi. "Keep your city life, Charlie, I'll take the country any day!"

Needless to say, we do have our history. Yet, because of that history, we are far ahead in some regards. One of the hot political issues of the state that often comes up was the issue of the state flag. Once again, I would remember a warning that my high school guidance counselor gave me when I told her I would attend Jackson State University. "You will learn to hate White folks if you go to that college." I did not understand her at the time.

One reason is because of the close relation-ships that I had with my fellow White friends in high school. For the most part, we lived on different sides of town. Both sides of town were largely poor, hard-working folks. We grew up together at school, played sports together, and our parents largely worked in the same factories. My high school years were as diverse as they could have been, though looking back we had separate Black and White proms, Black and White best dressed, Black and White class favorites, and the like. The problem was, we didn't know it was a problem, so it never was. We were just as happy for the White students who were elected as we were for the Black ones. After the big game, we all would get together in our separate groups and go visit the other groups to see what was going on over there. We had our fun on both sides of town. I guess the admini-strators somehow thought they were protecting us, or perhaps themselves. On Saturday nights, there was a place where the Whites hung out and there was a place where the Blacks hung out. Neither location was considered off grounds for either group. If we wanted to go see our White friends we knew exactly where to go, and the same was true of them.

So, when it came to the state flag of Mississippi, I never understood why I couldn't get dialed up about it. One of the things I learned was the moment you forget history, you are doomed to repeat it. For this reason, I thought, for better or worse, it was best to leave the state flag alone. Now, I must admit, I was probably in the minority on this view and didn't march to keep it flying high but my reasons were solid enough not to change my position. Let the rebels have their flag. It means something to them. At the time my position was this, "Find something that means something for you and stand up for it just as the rebel." Take it down and it means nothing! How can it mean nothing when it is a part of history? My thought was clear. Every symbol means something. Find out what it means to you and deal with it. Don't try to hinder what it may mean to someone else. For me, history was important. Even the most shameful moments in history take on different meanings for different folks. The good or bad of it all can point us to a better future. But if I forget why I dislike something because I no longer see it or if I forget why I love something because I no longer see it, what good is this?

On many national issues, we may find ourselves separated but one thing you will soon realize in Mississippi is that Black folks and White folks have been at this race thing for a long time. We know how to talk to each other, work with each other, and go to school with each other. That doesn't mean that we don't have areas of our state that are challenged in many of these same regards. Contrary to the many outside stereotypes of the state, you will find more friendships merged across racial lines in this state than you will enemies.

Culture is Not Racism:
Martin's Dream

Brotherly Love
"The sons of former slaves and the sons of former slave owners will be able to sit down together at the table of brother-hood."
(MLK, Jr. '63)

Cultural Diversity
"Little black boys and black girls will be able to join hands with little white boys and white girls as sisters and brothers."
(MLK, Jr. '63)

The Good White Folk
"For many of our white brothers, as
evidenced by their presence here today,
have come to realize that their destiny is
tied up with our destiny." (MLK, Jr. '63)

We Cannot Walk Alone
And as we walk, we must make the
pledge that we shall always march
ahead. We cannot turn back." (MLK,
Jr. '63)

Cultural differences are not always indicative of
racism. Cultural differences are an expression of who
a people are and have become because of experiences
and geographical locations endowed upon them by
Almighty God. The Confederate Southern heritage is
as legitimate and tangible as the Negro's demands for
certain foods rooted in his heritage. Let me be more
specific. I don't know a people in the annals of time
that love to eat hog chitterlings more so than the
Black man. When we gather to fill ourselves with the
delicacy of such delight, we are experiencing and
embracing deep cultural roots that are planted in our
history. I simply will not be denied my annual right to
indulge myself with as much of this God-given grace
than I can hold. On the other hand, my delight could
very well serve as disgust to some. Let them frown
and sneer at me as if I am inhuman to consume such

goods and I will simply have another bowl. You mess with a Black man's chitterlings and you will pay dearly! Now, we very well know that everything about this great prize is not good or healthy or even sane to prepare. However, certain times of the year, families will make their journeys to fulfill the ultimate quest of getting the best hog guts their money can buy. Certainly, all do not indulge. But it is unique to the Black man's story as much as the rebel flag and all of its history is to the Confederate heritage.

I don't compare apple and oranges. I compare heritage and culture. They are uniquely different for groups of people and they are expressed in various ways. A Flag has many meanings for different folks. That will never change. My ancestor was a servant under the Confederate flag. I can find no record of anything but admiration of that fact on his behalf. I suspect he would not have been the only one who would have had the experience of being a part of a war that would shake the history of our modern country.

No one can deny the existence of racism in America. Any institution that is governed to suppress and oppress a people cannot be labeled anything but what it is. Historians also understand that slavery was in existence throughout the world and was a practice in many societies. The United States of America was no exception. The overwhelming majority of my Confederate brothers and sisters agree that slavery was outright wrong. The Confederate flag does not indicate a racist any more than the cross indicates a Christian.

To suggest that having a White prom and a Black prom at one high school is racist is to not fully comprehend the important role of culture and the importance of race. That doesn't mean that we don't acknowledge that these practices may have derived from impure motives. Perhaps not so much today as it was in my day, Black folks and White folks listened to very different music, danced in very different ways, and had very different social norms. Again, this is not to deny that separation of races for such events, in former times, didn't have roots in racial identity and they may have evolved from racism. But to suggest that because these events were separate was inherently racist is wrong. As much as we loved our White classmates and were loved by them, we also loved our culture so much that we enjoyed our differences without allowing them to destroy our love for each other. Not to mention that at no time was anyone turned away from a White prom or a Black prom because they happened to show up at the wrong prom. We were genuinely happy to stop by each other's prom to share in the different cultural experience. This was well before we knew anything about cultural diversity. By some God-given desire, we were experiencing it. God made diversity and we have certainly had to grow to understand this over time. Perhaps it has been harder for one group to come to grips with this than another. However, now that we understand and value diversity and different cultural experiences, we now must embrace the old Southern Confederate culture as one that is as authentic and God given as any other. This is what has shaped a large segment of the Southern hospitality that is very common in this part of God's country among Blacks and Whites.

The Blacks that are descendants of the slaves who stayed in the South are as much part of this Confederate hospitality as anyone. What do we think happened to all of the culture the slaves absorbed in the South? Do we really think that all of the "soul food" in the South developed post-civil rights movement? What about the notion that Sunday dinner at Grandmother's house is a cultural norm of Black folks that started in the '70s? I contend that everything good about the South (Black and White) came from the old South just as much as anywhere else. This hospitality went north during the great migration of Negroes. Hard work, honesty, humility, strength, and integrity went north, as well. At the same time, a lot of it stayed south, close to the homeland.

Martin Luther King, Jr. had a dream before I was born that I would one day sit down with a Confederate brother and break bread at his table. I should not expect him to be any less of a Confederate than he is to expect me to be less Black. I have never sat on a red hill in Georgia but the red clay of Mississippi will do just fine. I think it is blissful that King would be able to see that the reunion of the slave master and the slave would occur in the immediate territory of their common ground. No new land would be established. Instead, new hearts would emerge in the same old land.

One of my first experiences of approaching my Confederacy came in the home of a patient that I cared for in rural Mississippi. There I was marveling at the distinct Southern culture that I found myself in. I knew right away that I was in deep cotton. Her husband was a true Confederate. The rebel flag flew high and the bumper sticker read, "Nathan Bedford Forrest." In my duties as a home health therapist, I have provided care for all kinds of people of different walks of life for the past six years. I know where the Confederates live and I know where the Black Nationalist lives.

This guy wasn't a lukewarm Confederate. He was true in his convictions and wasn't the kindest gentleman, but a gentleman indeed. He was a hard-shell Confederate. It must have been two weeks before I could get him to have a conversation. Part of the problem was it was election time and Barack Obama was running for his second term. I was a Black man in a Southerner's home with Fox News blasting anti-Obama lyrics. I was staring in the face of one of the meanest rebels I had ever met. I knew this one would be hard, so I decided to wait him out. He said nothing and neither did I. Meanwhile, that beautiful Southern lady and I carried on as if we had known each other for years. Being her therapist was a joy, but I must say,

I took note not to make her holler too much when stretching that shoulder. The old man was never really out of reach.

The final day came and I decided to go all in. I would break the silence in a way that I knew would either get me a solid scolding or would open up a deep dialogue. Up until this point, I had not disclosed my Confederate ties. I jumped right in when the door opened. It had become apparent to me that he was not going to turn Fox News off. I even think he turned it up when I walked through the door. I asked the question, "Who are they going to get to beat Obama this time? There is no way you good Southern Baptists are going to vote for a Mormon for president?"

Well, that did it. He jumped off that couch and that was the first time I had ever heard the term, "That Dang rag head!" He was referring to Obama, of course, and the silence was over. We talked politics, Civil War, and Nathan Bedford Forrest. At the time, I did not know that Forrest owned my ancestor. He disclosed to me his bitterness over land that his family had lost after the war. I could really feel his disgust in that regard. It was a victory for him and me. We had connected.

Using such a hot-button dagger as Obama in the home of a rebel was risky. However, I enjoyed it so much because it was the one weapon I held that I could use to break the hardest of the hard shells. It wasn't agreement that I sought. It was dialogue. I wanted to know more about the man. I am in the people business and there was no way I was going to leave that house without finding out more about who this man was and why. That to me completed the home health visit. It makes it whole. I'm glad I took that risk. It was several years later that I came to know that Nathan Bedford Forrest owned my great-great-grandfather. I returned to the home of this gentleman. But this dear brother had passed. I often wonder, had he known what I now know, what impact would that have had on our relationship, even as brief as it was?

There is much hope in Dr. King's dream. Black girls and boys would hold hands with White girls and boys. Is this not the hope of those that cry out for a post-racial America? However, there is an interpretation of Dr. King's dream here that I think is often overlooked. When I survey his dream, I see nothing that says the Black boy and girl would no longer be Black. I also see no indication that the White boy or girl wouldn't still be White. This is diversity at best. When people can be the people that God ordained them to be in their culture, they are at their best. Wrapped in the Confederate flag is a unique culture and heritage. I don't think I have any right to frown upon that heritage or culture any more than Confederates have a right to frown upon mine. I don't have to understand a person's culture or even agree with it in order to love them. Thus, because I am reconciled in Christ, I can allow a Confederate to be a Confederate without attacking him or her for their flag or their history. I can accept him as a Christian as much as any Christian in this land. After all, I am a part of that history. If the Jew could accept the Samaritan as a brother, who am I to not accept my Confederate brother? Moreover, my ancestor served under this banner with the pride of one doing his duty. I honestly believe he faithfully discharged those duties without prejudice and willingly. With honor, he and many other slaves stayed loyal to the Confederate nation.

My ancestor ties me directly to Confederate history in an odd and twisted way. That doesn't mean I condone slavery or wish that the Confederates had won the war to preserve slavery or establish a new nation. It just means that I am as complex as any man and the flag is one complex issue. To deny that it has been used as a symbol of hate is an outright lie. All of my Confederate friends agree to this fact and grieve this more than anyone. There is no pride in witnessing a symbol of pride and honor being used in a way that does not represent its meaning. Historically, some have taken the symbol of Christianity, the cross, and used it for warfare, cultism, slavery, and many other perversions contrary to its true meaning. Should we take down the cross because of the acts of the crusaders? Or should we rather study and learn from the crusades? I can find nowhere in the Bible that indicates that God hates history. In fact, I find just the opposite. It is HIS STORY. I believe a big part of HIS STORY is demonstrated in how well we seek the role of being our brother's keeper, which I will discuss in the last chapter. He often required monuments to remind Israel of their sin. God hates sin, not symbols. The symbol of sin is all around us but no one in our communities cry out against that as fiercely as they do against the Confederate flag. Unfortunately, this silence had led to mass incarceration due to drugs and homicides.

Revisionist history is taking your time horizon and historical perspective and applying it to the lens of time and history of a different era. By removing the original historical context from an object, position, or time and applying a new historical context that is specific to your time period is an incorrect way of interpreting history. Christians who are faithful to the Word of God understand this as they deal with scriptures. A proper method of understanding the scripture is to have a full grasp of the context and historical cultural narrative in which it is given. This is helpful to ensure that we receive God's Word and not our own as we apply it to our lives. To handle scripture any other way is a violation of the first principle of faithfully sharing the Word of God. Sadly, many Christians totally fail to apply this basic principle to American History and the Civil War. It is well known that men who used the Confederate battle flag symbol to portray supremacist views and bigotry as well as to suppress Black voters brought the flag of the Confederacy back into display in the era of the civil rights. The battle flag of the Confederate army had not flown since the end of the Civil War in 1865. Yet, bigotry resurrected the Confederate flag and forever stained a symbol that had been held in a time of war as a symbol of pride and honor for Blacks and Whites that served under it.

Just like the people in Enterprise, Alabama, erecting a monument to remind them of the one thing that brought destruction to their society, the Confederate flag helps to remind me of the painful history of African Americans as well as the unity that is offered by people who are willing to look at history as a tool for learning instead of an object of bitterness. It also reminds me of the high cost and sacrifice that Confederates, Whites and Blacks, endured for the building of this country. I have discovered that my Confederate brothers are not bent on putting Black folk back into slavery. In fact, it's just the opposite. They will look at you and tell you flat out that slavery was wrong. Yet, their ancestors, just like mine, fought in a war that had astronomical implications for our country. The fact that many were killed in this war means that they made the ultimate sacrifice that people can give of themselves for their country, right or wrong.

Now, we can certainly discuss and should discuss the facts of the Civil War. Did the Confederates lose the war, secede from the Union, fight for slavery versus state rights? And did slaves fight voluntarily or under compulsion for the South? Did Southerners or Northerners treat slaves better? I simply contend that there are too few African Americans who even consider these thoughts when they see a Confederate flag. Because history has been so cruel to our plight, we find ourselves without any useful historical regard to the Confederate flag. African Americans overwhelmingly have contempt of the flag because of the likes of Dylann Roof, the KKK, and the civil rights era. Hate groups taking the flag out of a larger historical context have hijacked the Confederate flag.

I remember the first time I heard President Obama speak. I had heard so much about this promising African-American guy named Obama. I had just received a phone call from a family member joking that whoever this guy Obama was he'd have to change his name because America would never elect a person with the last name Obama. Well, I had to see for myself. I finally caught the guy during a pre-election speech. I will never forget my response. I jumped off the couch and started running and yelling so loud that my family thought we had a burglar. I screamed in laughter and joy and said to my wife, "We haven't had a Negro speak like that since Martin Luther King, Jr. We have our first Black president!"

He had two beautiful young daughters at the time and my boys were excited that one-day they would get to meet them. I remember my youngest was fascinated. He asked if he could one day date the man's daughter.

I said, "Boy, what would you say to the President of the United States about dating his daughter?" His reply is in the annals of our family. He said. "I will tell him: Mr. Obama, I have a dream, too!" I said, "Boy, his name is Obama, not Martin Luther King, Jr."

We all laughed and told him that his reply would have been great.

Now, speaking of the president. I don't know one of my dear Confederate brothers who agree with anything that he has done. That's their right and their perspective. I can still love them, and laugh at them and with them. We usually come to the conclusion that we are really not too far off from each other on most issues. They mention Obama Care; I tell them to give me their Medicare card. They mention penalties, and I remind them that this was a Republican idea from the start (to tax people who weren't contributing to their cost). Ultimately, we come to one conclusion. Somehow, the politicians are getting richer but we are getting poorer. Once that point is reached, we are looking each other in the eye as men in the same boat.

But, what of the Confederate flag? Are we to remove it and take it down from every vestige of America's society? Only the great State of Mississippi remains. Should it be in a museum? Any serious student of history will find no better plight for the African American under the American flag as compared to the Confederate flag. We forget that it was the American flag that allowed slavery to thrive. For two centuries, *slavery existed in America under the American flag, not the Confederate flag.* We must pause to remember that at the time of the Underground Railroad, freedom was in Canada, not America. African Americans need to pause and think about that. The train stopped in Canada, not New York. And you will never see a KKK march without the prominent display of the American flag.

Robert E. Lee's Orderly: A Modern Black Man's Confederate Journey
Extended Edition

Make a Monument

"The monument did not showcase the boll weevil as the reason why the people of Enterprise couldn't succeed. It wasn't erected because they were displaying their excuse for failure for the world to see. It was simply saying, 'Here is what once was our problem. Here is the pest that pushed us to think different, to live different and as a result, to be successful.' (Enterprise Alabama, Coffee County erection of a monument to their problem, the Boll Weevil)

In order to inherit the promised land, the children of Israel had to cross over the Jordan River. There was no underground tunnel to cross the Jordan. The

Jordan River was, indeed, a problem. It was no little task ahead of them. We often forget that woman, children, elderly, and perhaps those who were handicapped had to cross. Four hundred years of oppression and it was time to cross this threshold of faith. What did God tell them to do? When you cross this river, don't ever remember it? Don't study it? Don't teach your children or mention this to them? Quite the contrary!

> Joshua 4:2
> "take twelve men out of the people, out of every tribe a man,"

> Joshua 4:3
> "And command ye them, saying, Take you hence out of the midst of Jordan, out of the place where the priests' feet stood firm, twelve stones, and ye shall carry them over with you, and leave them in the lodging place, where ye shall lodge this night."

- Make your monument out of your problems.
- Take the parts of the monument home with you.
- Place it near where you sleep.

Joshua 4:4
"Then Joshua called the twelve men, whom he had prepared of the children of Israel, out of every tribe a man,"

Joshua 4:5
"And Joshua said unto them, Pass over before the ark of the LORD your God into the midst of Jordan, and take ye up every man of you a stone upon his shoulder, according unto the number of the tribes of the children of Israel."

Your children are going to ask you later about your monument.

Joshua 4:6
"That this may be a sign among you, that when your children ask their fathers in time to come, saying, What mean ye by these stones?

Joshua 4:7
"Then ye shall answer them, That the waters of Jordan were cut off before the ark of the covenant of the LORD; when it passed over Jordan, the waters of Jordan were cut off: and these stones shall be for a memorial unto the children of Israel forever.

"These stones declared, 'There once was an obstacle in front of us that we couldn't get over. But God made a way. We never want to forget.'"

A biblical example of this is the rainbow. God left us a sign that he would never destroy the earth with water again. Out of the ugly destruction of His earth, He left a beautiful reminder to symbolize His promise. In some regard, I see the Confederate flag as that kind of symbol for me. I want to see it, if not daily, frequently, to remind me what God has done and that those days will never be seen again. On the other hand, the flag is a lasting tribute to my ancestor and his role in the war. Either way, to God be the glory.

African Americans need to start owning their history. We should make monuments instead of tearing them down. Instead of politicians, movie stars, and professional athletes tearing down history, they should be using their influence to build it up. History is important. It doesn't matter how you feel about it. History is objective, not subjective. The fact that Christ died on a cross over 2,000 years ago is an objective historical fact. It doesn't matter what you feel about it. Your feelings don't change that objective historical event. I don't ever want to forget my ancestors, my heritage, culture—our past. I don't ever want to forget the Civil War and those who fought in it. Before the 2014 movie *The Help* many young African Americans never knew the role of African-American women who were caring for White children in the '50s to '60s. African Americans need to understand that before *The Help* and *Driving Miss Daisy* of the '40s, '50s and '60s, there were the helpers and drivers of the Civil War and post-Civil War. This is the heritage that our movie stars and entertainers should be embracing. They should help to restore this vital part of our people's history and not relegate it as a thing of the past never to be remembered. I finally came to embrace this when, out of curiosity, I visited the website of The Sons of Confederate Camp in Mississippi. I was amazed at what level of interest the camp dedicated to "Black Confederates." At that moment, I had a subconscious understanding that these people couldn't possibly be against Black folks. The information on their website gave me a sense of comfort in knowing that my history would be valued instead of rejected. I just had one more step to take. I had to go see for myself. So, I went to the local relic show sponsored by the camp. This trip helped me to elevate my research to confirm what I had known since 2008. My thoughts were clear. If a White guy in Rankin County, Mississippi, could value the roles of Blacks in the Civil War, then certainly I had every right to do the same and even more so. To value the service of men and women who have been written out of this historical narrative could only be an honor. They were men like Turner Hall, Jr. who helped the Confederacy fight a war that lasted for four long and brutal years. These were men who helped build a country through their sacrifice. Why not build into this historical narrative? How about a movie about them? I think it is quite hypocritical for actors and actresses to make millions of dollars from the stories that they choose to play on the big screen and then turn around and attempt to use their influence in ways that will destroy the history of what has brought them fame. We have only seen a glimpse of the role that African Americans played in the Civil War through the movie, *Glory*. I would love to see a movie on Blacks' role in the war on both sides of the battle. Maybe that wouldn't be the politically correct thing to see but it would be historically accurate, to say the least. What is it about truth that makes it so hard to accept? Is it because we, too, have allowed our history to be hijacked by a certain era? Has our owned hatred and deep-rooted sin, anger, bitterness, and un-forgiveness caused us to blot out our own historical records? That's exactly what we are doing when we take the Confederate flag out of its entire context and make it a symbol of hate and racism. Ignorance can no longer be our way forward. For the sake of history and to honor the thousands of former slaves who served under the Confederate flag, I can't succumb to ignorance. History, the good, bad, and the ugly, are important.

Frederick Douglass stated of the Negroes in the South:

Frederick Douglass, Douglass' Monthly, IV [Sept. 1861], pp. 516: "there are at the present moment many colored men in the Confederate Army—as real soldiers, having muskets on their shoulders, and bullets in their pockets, ready to shoot down loyal troops, and do all that soldiers may do to destroy the Federal government. [. . .] There were such soldiers at Manassas and they are probably there still." ("Negroes in the Confederate Army," Journal of Negro History, Charles Wesle, Vol. 4, #3, [1919], 244–245)

Frederick Douglass stated of the Negroes in the North:

"The true history of this war will show that the loyal army found no friends at the South so faithful, active, and daring in their efforts to sustain the Government as the Negroes. It will be shown that they have been the safest guides to our army and the best pilots to our navy, and the most dutiful laborers on our fortifications, where they have been permitted thus to serve. It is already known that the tremendous slaughter of loyal soldiers at Pittsburgh Landing, where our army was surprised and cut to pieces, would have been prevented had the alarm given by a Negro, who had risked his life to give it, [had] been taken. The same is true of the destruction of the Maryland Regiment the other day at Port Royal. Gen. Burnside, in the difficult task committed to him of feeling his way into the intricate rivers and creeks of Virginia and North Carolina, had found no assistance among the so-called loyal whites comparable in value to that obtained from intelligent Black men. The folly and expense of marching an army to Manassas, after it had been evacuated more than a week, would have been prevented but for the contemptuous disregard of information conveyed by the despised men of color. Negroes have repeatedly threaded their way through the lines of the rebels exposing themselves to bullets to convey important information to the loyal army of the Potomac. Thousands of lives and millions of treasure might have been saved to the Government if these services had been appreciated by Commanding Generals. It was a Negro who struck the first terrible blow at rebel privatizing by killing the pirates and capturing the vessel, and today there is no man of the same opportunity so serviceable to the loyal army in South Carolina, as Robert Smalls, the colored pilot. The whites of the South, rich and poor, receive the loyal soldiers with sullen aversion, who the Blacks deem it their highest privilege to do them a service, although for doing so they have been delivered up by ungrateful officers to their rebel masters to suffer stripes and death. They seem determined to deserve credit whether they get it or not." (Fredrick Douglass, 1818–1895)

Frederick Douglass lays claim to the reality that Black men and slaves were not sitting idle with their arms folded watching White men fight. Slaves and free men of color were actively engaged in the Civil War on both sides and in many capacities. It is a mistake to think that there were not free men of color fighting in the Confederate army. This is the reality that I have come to accept. It is a reality that still awaits millions of modern African Americans.

Nathan Bedford Forrest:
The Good, Bad & the Ugly

General Nathan Bedford Forrest was the first grand wizard of the KKK. General Ulysses Grant called him, "that devil Forrest." It is noted that Tecumseh Sherman said of him, "The most remarkable man our Civil War produced on either side." At the end of the war, General Robert E. Lee was asked who was his best general. His reply, "That honor belongs to a general I have never met, Nathan Bedford Forrest." No other name would strike fear in the heart of Union commanders than his name. No one name would bring hope to the hearts of Confederates on the battle field than his name.

I will never forget the day I discovered my great-great-grandfather was owned by the family firm of Nathan Bedford Forrest. Because of my study of the Civil War and my quest to find out more about my ancestor's role as an orderly, I knew my generals on both sides of the conflict. Forrest was the one general that I didn't like. One of the things he was remembered for during the war was the Fort Pillow Massacre in Tennessee. Hundreds of Black soldiers and White officers were slaughtered after attempting to surrender. The term "no quarters" was heard on the battleground to signify the command to not take prisoners. It is debated among historians if Forrest had anything to do with the slaughter. Many Southerners, in order to protect his integrity, choose to deny that he had any responsibility for the killings. It is often said that his subordinates got out of control. The Fort Pillow Massacre has been a blemish on Forrest's military record since the war and even today is a highly contested issue. I personally think that Forrest was such a great General; he would have accepted full responsibility for any atrocities under his command. He wasn't a coward and didn't need defending on the battlefield. Because of this event and his brief association with the KKK, his image has suffered. I have named him the Twisted General. If I may, I will use modern Black slang to convey what I think has happened. It's the phrase, "Don't get it twisted."

I do believe Forrest has been twisted. On the one hand, he is given too much moral grace; and on the other hand, given way too much evil indignation.

The Civil War was a blood bath on many fronts. Like all humans, and he was human, many experiences are responsible for making us who we are. Not just the good ones, but the bad ones as well. Before I go into the twist of Forrest, let me tell you of my own...

Talking about a twist. I cannot tell you how twisted I was when I got the information from the Oklahoma Historical Society leading me to the knowledge that Nathan Bedford Forrest owned my great-great-grandfather. I was totally knocked down. He was the one Southern general that I had not warmed up to in all of my studies of the Civil War. Largely, the Fort Pillow Massacre had skewed my impression of the general. My eldest son attends Belmont University in Nashville, Tennessee. On visits to see him, I had refused to even look at the statue of Nathan Bedford Forrest on the interstate leading into the city of Nashville.

In preparation for our 15th annual Memorial Day weekend family reunion in Monroe County, Mississippi, I was doing family research on my ancestor, hoping to obtain new information. I was also preparing to share information on my ancestor at a local Sons of The Confederate Civil War relic show in June. The relic show, hosted by the Rankin Rough and Readys is widely attended. My mind was twisted, indeed. I knew of my ancestor's possible connection to General Lee. I also very well knew that he had not run away to the North or to join the Union. I knew that he had gone to the Gettysburg Black Diamond Reunion in 1938 as a Confederate representative. But, I had settled my mind, heart, and thoughts with these facts. This issue of being owned by Forrest—and the fact that he was still cherishing, at the age of ninety-five, the Confederate money given to him by Forrest—was just overwhelming.

I knew Forrest was a great general. I also knew of his association with the KKK. My uncles and relatives who grew up in the '50s and '60s, when the Klan was notorious against Blacks, would be present at the annual family reunion. I have strong nerves, but I wanted to shrink back from this one. I could see myself being burned at the stake at the family reunion in May and being hailed a hero at the Confederate show in June. How could this be?

I could not deny what was printed in the local *Oklahoman* on November 25, 1937. I read it over and over and over. And as they say in the South, I'll be, if it didn't say, Nathan Bedford Forrest.

I ran outside with chills over my body. I laughed and then I said, "Oh crap, this is crap!" I sat down again and read it again. It was no mistake. I had a *Good Times* Flo moment. "DANG, DANG, DANG FORREST!" (African Americans remember that day and know what I am talking about. It was the day the father of the family, James, died on the 1970s hit series, *Good-Times.*)

There he stood, my great-great-grandfather flanked between two young sons of the Confederate at ninety-five years old. A photo that no one in my family had ever laid eyes on. I didn't know whether to laugh or cry but I had to make up my mind soon. The family reunion and the Confederate relic show were right around the corner. I had to prepare to tell my huge family that the family firm of Nathan Bedford Forrest, a historically notorious figure, owned our ancestor. But if that was true, I had to know more about Forrest the man. Perhaps it would give me some insight into the mind of my ancestor. One thing about this new information that was clear to me was that my ancestor admired and cherished General Forrest.

After doing my homework on Forrest, this is what I have concluded, and this is what I conveyed to my family. General Nathan Bedford Forrest was like the one White boy back in the neighborhood who really could jump. You know, the one we grew up with that all the brothers were friends with because, at the end of the day, he could whip your butt. Like Larry Bird of basketball. All the brothers in my neighborhood loved the Lakers and the 76ers. Magic Johnson and Julius Irving (Dr. J) were doing some new things on the court that young Black boys dreamed of doing. However, there was still one dirty White boy always standing in the way. Larry Bird was that man on the court.

I was the only Boston Celtics fan on the school bus. We had multiple backyard stadiums in the neighborhood. Who won the last game on TV determined where we played the next sand-lock match. My Boston Garden was the host of many great games. I took the risk and it gave me plenty of bragging rights. Every Black person knows of at least one of these White boys. It's just better to be down with him because he is a beast. He could do stuff that no White boy was supposed to be able to do.

I remember playing football at Shannon High School. One of our rivalry teams, Pontotoc, had one of these White boys in the backfield. The scouting report was clear. One man couldn't take him and whatever you do, please don't hit him low. Well, I took the risk and got pummeled as Wesley Walls' cleats literally went over my facemask as he entered the end zone. Walls went on to have a stellar Pro Bowl career in the NFL. I saw him once hit a baseball straight up in the air and when the ball landed it was behind the center-field wall on the football practice field. It was a home run!

Well, Forrest only struck twice! One bad strike on the battlefield and one bad strike off the battlefield. Some would give him a third strike for his post-war activities. I don't. As painful as it is, history does not allow us to strip things out of context. If we do that, we might as well destroy the whole of humanity for the depravity that has existed from the fall of man.

Everything else that Forrest did was a home run. Put
that in perspective and you can maybe realize why he
is so respected over one hundred and fifty years later.

Forrest was the one general in the neighborhood that you didn't want to run into on the
battlefield. Out of fifty-four battles, he only lost one.
He had twenty-nine horses shot from under him
during the war. He was wounded eight times. He had
no formal military training but his tactics are still
studied today. He was just a backyard home-trained
rebel who fought with a purpose. Destroy the enemy!

His maneuvers at The Battle of Brice's
Crossroads are regarded by some military historians
as the single best military maneuvering of any general
in the history of our country. Many people can't grasp
the brutality of war. Anything other than that
perception of war is not reality. I have studied Fort
Pillow from both sides of the argument. I have
concluded that Blacks were there. They were there on
both sides of the battle. Unfortunately, many do not
realize that Forrest had Blacks with him at this battle.
At the end of the day, it was pure brutality. But that is
war. It brings me more validity to say that this is the
very reason why Blacks, regardless of what side of the
war they were on, should be commended. Any man
who is brave enough to take up arms and fight, or
brave enough to stand behind those who take up arms
and fight, is worthy of the respect and honor that only
a war can produce. When and if on the battlefield the

decision to kill or be killed is made, who am I to second-guess the thought of a man in the heat of a war? Even those who say it was a matter of policy before the battle to take "no quarters" for Blacks, policy doesn't read well when musket balls are flying high over your head. Needless to say, this is not the only example of such acts during the Civil War. A similar plight happened to Blacks at The Battle of Saltville, Virginia, when dozens of Black soldiers were dragged out of a hospital and killed.

People today talk about Forrest and Fort Pillow as if it was the only act that could have been considered a war crime. I found this report in the writings of the Black Scholar and trained Medical Physician, William Wells Brown, who was at the hospital for duties where the Black soldiers from Fort Pillow were taken in Cairo, Illinois. Brown writes, "It was told by a rebel officer that General Forrest shot one of his men, and cut another with his saber, who were shooting down prisoners." (Black Writers and The American Civil War Richard, Black Involvement and Participation in the War Between the States, Edited by Richard A Long page 39). This gives some insight into the fact that Forrest wasn't on the scene initially. It also provides a different take on his willingness to see surrendered Black or White soldiers murdered. On the other hand, the Union army was just as guilty of potential war crimes. Sherman's march on Atlanta saw the brutal treatment of Black slave women by his Union soldiers. What do you think the Northern general did when he saw these atrocities? Absolutely nothing.

In Osceola, Missouri, a pro-abolitionist political general, Senator James Lane, had nine military-age Southern men shot and killed for nothing other than they were suspected of aiding the Confederacy. What African Americans today need to understand is that slaves did whatever they could to survive and they caught hell doing it on both sides of the war. Yet, their bravery, chivalry, ingenuity, loyalty, and faith in God brought many through their trials.

There are other aspects of Forrest's character not known by many African Americans. One is that he is noted to be the first Southern White man to kiss Black women in public. He also has historically been known as one of the first White civil rights advocates. He was the first White man to be invited to speak before an all-Black pre-NAACP convention in 1875. Kissing Black women during the era of slavery certainly wasn't against the law. But to do so in public was not widely acceptable.

Forrest's gesture of embracing a Black woman in public was certainly not the norm. But Forrest was no normal Civil War General. He was not a military school General nor was he a political General. He was an uneducated, blue collar General, if you will. Nathan Bedford Forrest was a full man and a real warrior. Not a soft bone in his body and especially on the battlefield. Forrest, on July 5, 1875, embraced this Black woman at an organized event sponsored by The

Independent Order of Pole-Bearers Association. This organization was the predecessor to the NAACP.

"Ladies and Gentlemen, I accept the flowers as a memento of reconciliation between the white and colored races of the Southern states. I accept it more particularly as it comes from a colored lady, for if there is any one on God's earth who loves the ladies I believe it is myself. (Immense applause and laughter.) I came here with the jeers of some white people, who think that I am doing wrong. I believe I can exert some influence, and do much to assist the people in strengthening fraternal relations, and shall do all in my power to elevate every man to depress none. I want to elevate you to take positions in law offices, in stores, on farms, and wherever you are capable of going. I have not said anything about politics today. I don't propose to say anything about politics. You have a right to elect whom you please; vote for the man you think best, and I think, when that is done, you and I are freemen. Do as you consider right and hones in electing men for office. I did not come here to make you a long speech, although invited to do so by yours. I am not much of a speaker, and my business prevented me from preparing myself. I came to meet you as friends, and welcome you to the white people. I want you to come nearer to us. When I can serve you, I will do so. We have but one flag, one country; let us stand together. We may differ in color, but not in sentiment [. . .] many things have been said about me which are wrong, and which white and black persons here, who stood by me through the war, can contradict. Go to work, be industrious, live honestly, and act truly, and when you are oppressed I'll come to your relief. I thank you, ladies and gentle-men, for this opportunity you have afforded me to be with you, and assure you that I am with you in heart and in hand. (Prolonged applause.) (General Nathan Bedford Forrest, July 5, 1875)

Whereupon, Nathan Bedford Forrest again thanked Miss Lewis for the bouquet and then gave her a kiss on the cheek. Such a kiss was unheard of in the society of those days, in 1875, but it showed a token of respect and friendship between the general and the Black community and did much to promote harmony among the citizens of Memphis. (Tennessee- SCV.org)

General Forrest was also a man who evoked deep loyalty from his slaves. When the war started, General Forrest took forty-five slaves with him to battle. At the end of the war, all but one stood with him. It is reported that he informed the slaves at the onset that they would be fighting for their freedom. If the South lost, they would be set free. If the South won the war, he would set them free. Either way, they would be free. Forrest bestowed honor upon these men as among the bravest Confederate soldiers as any in his camp. Furthermore, it is noted that in his handpicked inner circle of the best Cavalrymen that he possessed, at least eight were slaves.

"I said to 45 colored fellows on my plantation that I was going into the army; and if they would go with me, if we got whipped they would be free anyhow, and that if we succeeded and slavery was perpetrated, if they would act faithfully with me to the end of the war, I would set them free. Eighteen months before the war closed I was satisfied that we were going to be defeated, and I have those 45, or 44 of them, their free papers for fear I might be called." (General Nathan Bedford Forrest, Congressional Testimony after the war).

In late August of 1868, General Nathan Bedford Forrest gave an interview to a reporter. Forrest said of the Black men who served with him: "These boys stayed with me…and better Confederates did not live." (Forrest, 1868)

Black Private Louis Napoleon Nelson served the Confederate states of America at Shiloh, Lookout Mountain, Brice's Crossroads and Vicksburg as soldier and chaplain in the 7th Tennessee Cavalry, under Lt. General Nathan Bedford Forrest.

Col. Parkhurst's (Northern) Account of Forrest's Black Confederates:

The forces attacking my camp were the First Regiment Texas Rangers, a battalion of the First Georgia Rangers… and quite a number of Negroes attached to the Texas and Georgia troops, who were armed and equipped and took part in the several engagements with my forces during the day." (Lieutenant Colonel Parkhurst's Report, Ninth Michigan Infantry, on General Forrest's attack at Murfreesboro, Tennessee, July 13, 1862, in official Records, Series I, Vol XVI, Part I, page 805)

God's Salvation

It came in the fall of 1875 prior to Forrest's presentation at the Independent Order of Pole-Bearers Association meeting. Reverend George Tucker Stainback preached from these Holy Words:

"Everyone then who hears these words of mine and does them will be like a wise man who built his house on the rock. And the rain fell, and the floods came, and the winds blew and beat on that house, but it did not fall, because it had been founded on the rock. And everyone who hears these words of mine and does not do them will be like a foolish man who built his house on the sand. And the rain fell, and the floods came, and the winds blew and beat against that house, and it fell, and great was the fall of it." (Matthew 7:24–27)

In the pews that day was Nathan Bedford Forrest. According to Rev. Stainback, Forrest said to him, "Sir, your sermon has removed the last prop from under me. I am the fool that built on the sand. I am a poor miserable sinner."

The Reverend gave Forrest the challenge of reading these words in the privacy of his home:

"Have mercy on me, O God, according to your steadfast love; according to your abundant mercy blot out my transgressions. Wash me thoroughly from my iniquity, and cleanse me from my sin! For I know my transgressions, and my sin is ever before me." (Psalm 51:1–3)

The preacher followed up with Forrest the next day and they prayed together as Forrest accepted his Redeemer. On his dying bed, two years later, Forrest said, "There is no cloud that separates me from my Heavenly Father."

What God-fearing Christian man or women today would deny that God's salvation did not come to Nathan Bedford Forrest on that fall day in 1875? If any Christian declares that this is not salvation, as we know the scriptures to teach, then he stands to be judged as the man who built his house upon sand. If you say this is not a biblical understanding of faith in

Christ by Grace, you are standing in your own salvation and not that of God. The beauty of salvation is in God, not the sinner. How beautifully did He call this dear brother to Himself through His preached Word! He shall call all of His children to this marvelous light. And they will be redeemed for His glory.

Any man who denies God's salvation of Nathan Bedford Forrest and refuses to allow this great military general and redeemed soul to rest in peace and with honor must also deny all of John Newton's hymn, *Amazing Grace*, and all of the writings of Apostle Paul. Newton was a slave trader of the most serious kind. Apostle Paul persecuted Christians to the point of death. They both heard a cry from heaven by the same Holy Spirit that saved Nathan Bedford Forrest. Like Forrest, scales fell from their eyes. They realized that they, too, were standing on sand. They repented of their sins and we now enjoy the wonderful blessings of God's redemption of these two souls. It is time for Black Christians to acknowledge the same grace for Forrest or forever cease to sing the great Christian hymn written by a former slave trader. To deny this hymn in our worship of God would fundamentally change the Black church forever. There is not one African-American Church in this country that doesn't know a former slave trader gave this great hymn to us, the body of Christ. How ironic, the president of these great United States and our African-American political hero led the Church in South Carolina in song by using the hymn of John Newton, a former slaver. This hymn was a main source of comfort and unifying force among Blacks and Whites attending the funeral of Pastor Clementa Pinckney. All of America, if not the world, witnessed triumph over evil, hatred and sin through this song. How is it that we can afford forgiveness to this brother, Newton, and not extend it to our brother Forrest? Do we have scales on our eyes? Was Newton any less of a sinner than Forrest? Was Apostle Paul? No! These men were no more sinner than any man! Yet, like Apostle Paul, Forrest claimed himself to be the worst of sinners.

Therefore, are we to deny the writings of the great Apostle Paul? God forbid! This is why I now gaze upon the Nashville statue of Forrest with tears in my eyes. I rest upon a monument and testimony to the great Grace of God. This is what Turner Hall, Jr. knew and understood about grace. This is why, seventy-two years after the Civil War, he could be found professing possessions given to him by General Forrest as his most prized. For he, too, was a sinner saved by this same marvelous grace. It also speaks to how he must have thought about Forrest even during the war. May Forrest's remembrance, like that of John Newton and Apostle Paul, forever challenge us of our own sin and remind us what is ours through faith in Christ, our great and Almighty God. If the Black and White folks who think Forrest's and other Civil War monuments are to be destroyed, it is because they don't rightly see grace or the value of honoring and remembering the greatness of these generals and their value to history, both good and bad. Give me the remains of the greatest military general in the history of our country, Nathan Bedford Forrest, and I will build a monument in the heart of downtown Jackson, Mississippi and revitalize a dilapidated community by establishing the largest Civil War museum in this country. We could use the proceeds from such site to restore this community. We could educate our children on our past so that they learn factual truths about history and what role our people played in it. In fact, Jackson, Mississippi, has enough Civil war history and Black history of that era to underwrite the best-paved streets in the country. Yet, we rather settle on our elderly poor paying high water bills and taxes to patch our roads. We pat ourselves on the back as if we are progressing. As we say in the great state of Mississippi, "Hogwash!" We don't look to build on our rich history to attract people from all over the world to see. We put our heads in the holes of history and continue to cripple our people with ignorance. Instead of using our history to unite us, we fall into the trap of an unforgiving spirit and a bitterness that separate us from our rich history and valuable resources.

Finally, back to that confederate money. In my mind, there are three possibilities to explain how my ancestor had Confederate money given to him by General Forrest. Confederate monies were issued between 1861-1865. The first possibility that I had to consider was that it could have been given to him for his service as one of Forrest's forty-five slaves who served with him. I don't hold to this first possibility for two reasons. First, I found no documentation to support that he was numbered among the forty-five slaves whom Forrest took to war with him. Another reason is that it is documented that he served as a body servant for two non-commissioned Confederate soldiers. The second possibility was that General Forrest could have presented Turner, Jr. with the Confederate money after the war. I don't find anything that states that this didn't happen, but it just doesn't seem plausible considering the money at that point was worthless. However, if this second possibility is correct, it would take on more meaning, signifying an even deeper relationship among the two men. It would be similar to two old friends getting together for a beer after a long hard struggle and one giving the other a keepsake as a token of something to be remembered for the good ol' times. Although this view is very possible, I tend to lean to the third alternative. The money was given to him as part of a dynamic relationship that had been forged between the slave master and the slave. If you take into account that Bedford Forrest took forty-five of his slaves with him at the onset of the war (and I don't consider my great-great grandfather to be one of them) then it is my estimate that he would have been owned by Forrest before the war started. Moreover, Forrest had a reputation of being kind toward his slaves and taking good care of them. This leads me to believe that during his role as a body servant for two Confederate soldiers, he would have come into contact with his former master and obtained this monetary gift during the war in passing between a former master and slave. Taking into account that General Robert E. Lee and General Forrest never met during the war, this opens up the idea that Turner would have traveled with his Confederate comrades throughout the theater of the war and at some point been introduced to General Robert E. Lee. At that point, he would have assumed duties of caretaker for Lee's horse Traveller, among other things based upon a recommendation. I gather he was likely introduced to Lee as "one of Bedford's slaves." If you consider Lee's admiration for Bedford Forrest, Bedford's reputation of having very loyal slaves as a result of being a good master, as well as Turner's prior superb service to two Confederate soldiers, a recommendation to General Lee would have been all he needed to gain clearance to be numbered worthy as one of General Lee's servants.

I am convinced now more than ever that Turner Hall, Jr. and Nathan Bedford Forrest are in the same heaven. They have now, at this moment, more friendship than they ever could have had on earth. How sweet would it be if the descendants from their generation could abide in the same love? Only in Christ are we able to see that their lives and their history affords us this wonderful opportunity

The Mystical Black Confederate

Mystery and mystic surrounds the Black Confederate. Some would be so cynical to say there's even a mythical suspense around the idea of a Black Confederate. This idea of a Black Confederate is one of the last great battles of the Civil War. Perhaps the greatest is the battle between States Rights and Slavery.

The Black Confederate battle is similar to many of the Civil War battles during the war. You have these two giant foes, the White Northerner and the White Southerner tussling in the dynamic midst of a society that doesn't just involve them. And yet, only glimpses in the historical accounts of the Black Confederate exist. Thus, in the backdrop of this great battle, there are silent voices, strong arms and mighty forces that are engaged in ways that create ongoing anxiety, curiosity and suspense in the hearts and minds of the enemies of battle as they confront the intrigue and mystique throughout the post war era. The farther we get away from the war, the greater the mystique. To be mystical is to have a spiritual meaning of reality that is neither apparent to the senses or obvious to the intellect. There is no greater example of this definition than the Black Confederate. He spoils the senses of the brain and defies the mental capacity of modern thinkers.

Imagine, if you will, the notion of forces un-known by either side that appears in spurts of great or lesser ferocity over the course of a four year war. It reminds me of the mystical powers of Jim Beckwourth, one of the first Black American Frontiersmen who became Chief of the Crow Nation. Jim would use his machinations not only to bewilder his foe but to his companions at bay so much so that the very sight of him would astonish onlookers with awe.

The Black Confederate is a quandary of belief or disbelief surrounded around these mystical drops of lore that are handed down throughout history with more recent deliverance of accounts established by the will of men, such as myself, who resurrect the stories of Blacks who served in the Confederate armies. Much is done to suppress these stories at the expense of reducing the Black Confederate to no more than a camp slave less the grand epic battle of Slavery as the cause of the war is lost.

Since a child, I have been fascinated with people who report sightings of the Sasquatch. Is he mythical or not? Every man will have to decide for himself on the Sasquatch. However, in regard to the Black Confederate, there is something inherently unique to him that sets him apart from myth and mystery. It doesn't resolve his mystical being but it places him squarely in the realm of reality. It's something that is inherent and tangible and often can't be explained. This inherent ability of human relationships is rooted in us from creation and sets each human as an independent guardian of the stewardship to protect, guard, love or value your fellow man. Relationships between human beings are one of the most powerful forces that God grants to man in being like Him. The height of this dynamics is displayed between men and women in marriage. It is such a force that it is described as one flesh, the two shall become one.

The doubters and skeptics of Black Confederate usually account for their position based upon the Confederate's official military record of refusing to arm slaves or free people of color or the lack of Confederate muster rolls providing an account of the names, positions and rank of Blacks. Where the skeptics fall terribly short is in the realm of reality that is indicative of the human relationships. Though man's inherent willingness is always bent toward himself, the unquenchable capacity to establish deep abiding relationships with other humans is universal. Consider-ing the Black Confederate, the absolute skeptics (those that allow no room for a single Black Confederate) wrestle against a God that cannot be boxed in by a framework that suits man's narrative. You see, they literally throw the babe out with the bath water. This is not hard to imagine if you consider it's not the first time relationships played a role in a determining factor regarding Blacks in Warfare. During the American Revolutionary War, the British offered scores of Blacks their freedom if they fought against their colonies. They refused and joined the rag tag militias that succeeded in America's Independence. One such slave, Salem Poor, at the Battle of Bunker Hill received 14 letters of commendation from the legislature in Massachusetts praising him as a, "Brave and Gallant Soldier" deserving of an award.

Here lies the height of the hypocrisy of those Yankees who fight at all cost to deny the Black Confederate existence. For some reason, he thinks it's honorable for his slave or the free Black to fight during the American Revolution for the land and relationships that he knew as home but doesn't allow that same claim for the free or slave Black in the South. Any casual study of history will find Blacks who were free and enslaved fight at the Battle of Bunker Hill, Lexington and Concord. How is it that it's more honorable for a Northern slave to fight than a Southern Slave? The Royal Governor of Virginia wanted to divide and conquer by offering the Blacks their freedom. Washington, just like Lincoln, reluctantly raised a "Black Regiment of the 1st Rhode Island". And just like the Negro during the Civil War who fought on either side, theirs wasn't a harder fighter than the "Black Regiment of the 1st Rhode Island" one British commander resigned his commission instead of facing these men in battle. What happened to the muster rolls of these men? They were destroyed just like the records of the Confederates. The roles of Blacks in war have always been suppressed until recent history. That's just a fact of history. The fact doesn't give anyone permission to deny any existence of their service. Let's remember the record. On March 5, 1770 five colonist were killed by British Troops in Boston Massachusetts in the infamous event known as the "Boston Massacre." The first of them was a Black man name Crispus Attucks. From this event, America was born!

The real reality for the "Never Black Confederate" movement is rooted in a concept of ultimate denial of the Creator's sovereign ability to do things that are incomprehensible to us through relationships. Yet, the Creator is all about relationships. By disallowing any grace toward their Southern counterpoints, their denial is not to protect, honor, love or shield Blacks from any disgrace. Their denial is one of moral aptitude of the haughtiest disposition against the means of grace that God affords everyman or women, to enter into relationships and fellowship with his fellow man. Every man or women who has ever been in an actual war would readily tell you how quickly these relationships are sealed after the first bullets start to fly over your head and you are reduced to a mere mortal.

HOLT COLLIER

The Great Mystical Black Confederate, Holt Collier: Born a slave in Greenville, Mississippi in 1848. He is known to have killed more bears than Daniel Boon and David Crockett combined killing his first at the age of 10.

In order to join his boyhood companion, Tom Hinds, Holt found shelter on a riverboat and joined Tom in the War. Although the position of the Confederate army wasn't to enroll Black Soldiers, the exception was granted to Holt and he served through the war as a Confederate Soldier. His journey lead him to be attached to Company I of the 9th Texas Cavalry. Holt saw action in several Southern States. After the war, he contributed to the famous bear hunt by President Teddy Roosevelt throughout the Mississippi Delta in 1902.

Once, Holt successfully cornered a Black bear, Roosevelt was unable to bring himself to shoot the animal leading to a national cry of him being a "Teddy Bear." Holt had tied the bear to a tree for the President to kill but his will to do so escaped him at the moment of conquest. From this hunt, the Black Confederate delivered the famous "Teddy Bear" to the world. Holt has a 1400 acre National Wildlife Reserve named in his honor in Mississippi.

AN EARLY SIGHTING

The Mystical Black Confederate seen as early as 1861! Notice in the account how he is described as this mystical "New Feature" that was "Positively identified!"

"Yesterday morning General Mansfield with Drake de Kay, Aide-de-Camp in command of seven companies of the 20th New York, German Riffles, left Newport News on a reconnaissance. Just after passing Newmarket Bridge, seven miles from camp, they detached one company as an advance, and soon after their advance was attacked by 600 of the enemy's cavalry.

The company formed to receive cavalry, but the CAVALRY ADVANCING deployed to the right and left when within musket range and unmasked a body of SEVEN HUNDRED negro infantry, all armed with muskets, who opened fire on our men, wounding two lieutenants and two privates, and rushing forward surrounded the company of Germans who cut their way through killing six of the negroes and wounding several more.

The main body, hearing the firing, advanced at a double-quick in time to recover their wounded, and drive the enemy back, but did not succeed in taking any prisoners. The wounded men TESTIFY POSITIVELY that they were shot by Negroes, and that not less than seven hundred were present, armed with muskets.

This is, indeed, a new feature in the war. We have heard of a regiment of Negroes at Manassas, and another at Memphis, and still another at New Orleans but did not believe it till it came so near home, and attacked our men. THERE IS NO MISTAKE ABOUT IT. The 20th German were actually attacked and fired on and wounded by Negroes.

It is time that this thing was understood, and if they fight us with Negroes, why should not we fight them with Negroes too? We have disbelieved these reports too long, and now let us fight the devil with fire. The feeling is intense among the men. They want to know if they came here to fight Negroes, and if they did, they would like to know it. The wounded men swear they will kill any Negro they see, so excited are they at the dastardly act. It remains to be seen how long the Government will now hesitate, when they learn these facts. One of the Lieutenants was shot in the back part of the neck, and is not expected to live."

Sandusky Ohio Register
December 31, 1861
Above From:
Indianapolis Journal December 23, 1861

FREE NEGRO, LEVIN GRAHAM. A RARE MYSTICAL SIGHTING

Levin Graham, a free colored man, was employed as a fifer, and attendant to Captain J. Welby Armstrong (2nd Tennessee). He refused to stay in camp when the regiment moved, an obtaining a musket and cartridges, went across the river with us. He fought manfully, and it is known that he killed four of the Yankees, from one of whom he took a Colt's revolver. He fought through the whole battle, and not a single man in our whole army fought better" *(New Orleans Daily Crescent, 6 December 1861)*

THE MYSTICAL BLACK CONFEDERATE SEAMAN, LAWRENCE GRAVES

It is known that Confederate Naval Records and Confederate State Marine Records were destroyed at the end of the War. It's not uncommon for the defeated army to destroy records to prevent them from falling into the hand of the enemy. Many claim that Body Servants didn't fire weapons. Confederate Lawrence Graves, a body servant of Lieutenant Henry Graves, C.S, Marine Corps was one that proves this claim to be untrue.

The brother of Lieutenant Graves wrote a letter home to family and stated, "Lawrence was much elated with the idea of having shot at some Yankees before evacuation and thinks he hit one." *(Richard Harrell (ed.), A Confederate Marine: (Tuscaloosa AL: Confederate Pub. Co., Inc., 1963), 126-127 & 129)*

MOSES DALLAS

"A letter from his Squad Commander to the Secretary of the Navy says, "I have also been compelled to increase the pay of Moses Dallas from $80 to $100 per month in order to retain him. He is a colored pilot and is considered the best inland pilot on the coast." Moses died along with five of his Confederate comrades in June of 1864 in a battle for the Union gunboat, the USS Water Witch, which the Confederates succeeded in Capturing. *(Northern Official Records Vol 15, 468-506, N.O.R. vol. 15, 704 & 708)*

TUCKER'S BRIGADE

Tucker's Marine Brigade (Commodore John R. Tucker) captured three days before the Appomattox Surrender had three Blacks, Charley Cleaper, James Hicks and Joe Johnson). Although surrounded by six Union Division at the Battle of Sayler's Creek, these three men escaped and rejoined the Army of Northern Virginia. At the surrender, they were listed among Tucker's Brigade with rank of "Private."

Tucker's Brigade fought the six Union Division so fierce that the Union officers estimated 2,000 when in reality they only numbered between 300-400 Confederates. *(Roll of the C.S. Naval Brigade surrendered at Appomattox, VA, April 9-10 1865, 266 Reels 5 & 6, Microcopy 260, U.S. National Archives)*

MARTIN JACKSON

"I was here in Texas when the Civil War was first talked about. I was here when the War started and followed my young master into it with the First Texas Cavalry [Confederate State of America]. I was here during reconstruction, after the War. I was here during the European World War [1914-1918] and the second week after the United States declared war on Germany I enlisted as cook at Camp Leon Springs. This sounds as if I liked the war racket. But, as a matter of fact, I never wore a uniform grey coat or khaki coat or carried a gun, unless it happened to be one worth saving after some Confederate soldier got shot. I was official lugger-in of men that got wounded, and might have been called a Red Cross worker if we had had such a corps connected with our company. My father was head cook for the battalion and between times I helped him out with the mess. There was some difference in the food served to soldiers in 1861 and 1917!

Just what my feelings was about the War, I have never been able to figure out myself. I knew the Yanks were going to win, from the beginning. I wanted them to win and lick us Southerners, but I hoped they was going to do it without wiping out our company. I'll come back to that in a minute. As I said, our company was the First Texas Cavalry. Col. Buchel was our commander. He was a full-blooded German and as fine a man and a soldier as you ever saw. . . Lots of old slaves closes the door before they tell the truth about their days of slavery. When the door is open, they tell how kind their masters was and how rosy it all was. You can't blame them for this, because they had plenty of early discipline, making them cautious about saying anything uncom-plimentary about their masters. I, myself, was in a little different position than most slaves and, as a consequence, have no grudges or resentment.

However, I can tell you the life of the average slave was not rosy. They were dealt out plenty of cruel suffering. It was in the Battle of Marshall, in Louisiana, that Col. Buchel got shot. I was about three miles from the front, where I had pitched up a kind of first-aid station. I was all alone there. I watched the whole thing. I could hear the shooting and see the firing. I remember standing there and thinking the South didn't have a chance. All of a sudden, I heard someone call. It was a soldier, who was half carrying Col. Buchel in. I didn't do nothing for the Colonel. He was too far gone. I just held him comfortable, and that was the position he was in when he stopped breathing. That was the worst hurt I got when anybody died. He was a friend of mine." *(MARTIN JACKSON, Confederate army: First Texas Cavalry; enslaved in Texas, interviewed in Texas, 1937 WPA Slave Narrative Project, Federal Writers' Project, U.S. Work Projects Administration (USWPA).*

GUS BROWN

"Then de war came and we all went to fight the Yankees. I was a body servant to the master, and once a bullet took off his hat. We all thought he was shot but he wasn't, and I was standin' by his side all the time. I remember Stonewall Jackson. He was a big man with long whiskers, and very brave. We all fought wid him until his death. We wan't beaten. We wuz starved out! Sometimes we had parched corn to eat and sometimes we didn't have a bite o' nothin', because the Union mens come and tuck all the food for their selves.

I can still remember part of my ninety years. I remembers we fought all de way from Virginia and winded up in Manassah's

Gap. When time came for freedom most of us wuz glad. We liked the Yankees. They was good to us. "You is all now free." "You can stay on the plantation or you can go." We all stayed there until old massa died. Den I worked on de Seaboard Airline [Railroad] when it come to Birmingham. I have been here ever since.

In all de years since de war I cannot forget old massa. He was good and kind. He never believed in slavery but his money was tied up in slaves and he didn't want to lose all he had. I knows I will see him in heaven and even though I have to walk ten miles for a bite of bread I can still be happy to think about the good times we had then. I am a Confederate veteran but my house burned up wid de medals and I don't get a pension." *GUS BROWN, Confederate army; enslaved in Virginia, interviewed in Alabama, 1937. WPA Slave Narrative Project, Federal Writers' Project, U.S. Work Projects Administration (USWPA).*

ALBERT JONES
"When I wuz twenty one, me and one of my brothers run away to fight wif the Yankees. Us left Souf Hampton county and went to Petersburg. Dere we got some food.

Den us went to Fort Hatton where we met some more slaves who had done run away. When we got in Fort Hatton, us had to cross a bridge to git to de Yankees. Dey give us food and clothes.

Yer know, I was one of de first colored cavalry soljers, and I fought in Company "K." I fought for three years and a half. Sometimes I slept out doors, and sometimes I slept in a tent. De Yankees always give us plenty of blankets.

During the war some un us had to always stay up nights and watch fer de rebels. Plenty of nights I has watched, but de rebels never 'tacked us when I was on.

Not only wuz dere men slaves dat run to de Yankees, but some un de women slaves followed dere husbands. Dey use to help by washing and cooking.

One day when I was fighting, de rebels shot at me, and dey sent a bullet through my head. I wuz lucky not to be kilt. Look. See how my hand is? But dat didn't stop me, I had it bandaged and kept on fighting.

The uniform dat I wore wuz blue wif brass buttons; a blue cape, lined wif red flannel, black leather boots and a blue cap. I rode on a bay color horse fact every body in Company "K" had bay color horses. I tooked my knap-sack and blankets on de horse back. In my knap-sack I had water, hard tacks and other food.

When de war ended, I goes back to my mastah and he treated me like his brother. Guess he wuz scared of me 'cause I had so much ammunition on me. My brother, who went wif me to de Yankees, caught rheumatism doing de war. He died after de war ended. (*ALBERT JONES, Union army: Ninth Cavalry, Company K; enslaved in Texas, interviewed in Virginia, ca. 1937 WPA Slave Narrative Project, Federal Writers' Project, U.S. Work Projects Administration (USWPA).*

ANDRE CALLIOUX, A UNION GIANT

The Mystical Black Union Officer and Hero, Andre Callioux at the Battle of Port Hudson. Callioux was the first African American Union Officer killed in the Civil War. Colonial Douglass Wilson in a 1890 interview said of Callioux, "If ever patriotic heroism deserved to be honored in stately marble or in brass that of Captain Callioux deserves to be, and the American people will have never redeemed their gratitude to genuine patriotism until that debt is paid."

His actions were described by Rodolphe Desdunes, whose brother, Aristide, served under Callioux: "The eyes of the world were indeed on this American Spartacus. The hero of ancient Rome displayed no braver heroism than did this officer who ran forward to his death with a smile on his lips and crying, "Let us go forward, O comrades!" Six times he threw himself against the murderous batteries of Port Hudson, and in each assault, he repeated his urgent call, "Let us go forward, for one more time!" Over 3,000 attended his funeral.

JAMES CAPE

"One day Marster Bob comes to me and says, "Jim, how you like to jine de army?" You see, de war had started. I says to him "What does I have to do?" And he says, "Tend hosses and ride 'em." I was young den and thought it would be lots of fun, so I says I'd go. So de first thing I knows, I's in de army away off east from here, somewhar dis side of St. Louis and in Tennessee and Arkansas and other places. I goes in de army 'stead of Dr. Carroll.

After I gits in de army, it wasn't so much fun, 'cause tendin' hosses and ridden' wasn't all I done. No, sari, I has to do shoot in' and git shooter at! One time we stops de train, takes Yankee money and lots of other things off dat train. Dat was way up de other side of Tennessee.

You's heard of de battle of Independence? Dat's whar we fights for three days and nights. I's not tendin' hosses dat time. Dey gives me a rifle and sends me up front fightin', when we wasn' runnin'. We does a heap of runnin' and dat suits me. I could do dat better'n advance. When de order comes to 'treat, I's all ready.

I gits shot in de shoulder in dat fight and lots of our soldiers gits killed and we loses our supply." (*JAMES CAPE, Confederate army; enslaved in Texas, interviewed in Texas, ca. 1937*

WPA Slave Narrative Project, Federal Writers' Project, U.S. Work Projects Administration (USWPA).

Turner Hall, Jr., October 10, 1840- January 5th, 1942
(Family Photo)

Pappa Turner

The Mystical Orderly of Robert E. Lee,
Turner Hall, Jr.
Route 1, Box 207-A
Pierce City, MO 65723
March 20, 1983

"Mr. R. E. Jackson of Aberdeen,
Mississippi has suggested that I write to you
for information regarding Turner Hall who
died in 1942.

Let me introduce myself and explain the
reason for this long letter. I am now a retired
government worker from Washington, D.C. I
have been a writer all my life and now write
about six magazine articles a year. When I was
graduated from school in 1938, one of my first

jobs was editor of the daily newspaper at Hugo, Oklahoma. It was there that I first met Turner Hall who at that time was a fine old man who was nearly 100 years old who liked to talk about General Lee and how he, Turner Hall, took care of the General's horse, Traveler. I remember that he went to New York City in April, 1940, and was interviewed on the CBS nationwide radio show "We, the People."

In the autumn of 1940 I left Hugo to enter the military service. In 1980, some 40 years later, the editor of a children's magazine was interested in a story about Black history, and I suggested the Turner Hall story. Needless to say, I have never written the story because I have been unable to gather the necessary information for it. After a 40-year absence I returned to Hugo and found that the old generation was gone and the new generation knew little or nothing about the pre-World War II period. The old newspaper files had been destroyed and the CBS network headquarters in New York City reported that the transcript of Turner Hall's interview was not available. I began a search for (type faded) but did not know where to start. I could not find any funeral home in Hugo, and I had no idea in what year Turner Hall died. I searched the cemeteries for a grave marker, with no success. So many of the graves"... 2nd page of letter lost. (Mystery Writer, letter to family, March 20, 1983)

For years it remained a mystery letter. Placed in our family heritage book with the caption, "A letter to Sammie Hall, Sr. with someone searching for information about Turner Hall." The family lost the second page of the letter dated March 20, 1983, from Pierce City, Missouri. This mystery writer was inquiring about the final whereabouts of Turner Hall. It wasn't until 2014 that I discovered the name of the writer.

This unexpected gift happened when I became brave enough to snoop around the doorstep of my Confederacy. I wanted to gauge the degree of my reception or rejection of my fellow Confederate brethren. There was no better way for me to find out that to go to a place where I knew Confederates would be in abundance, the relic show. To my pleasure, my time was filled with sincere welcomes and open doors. Southern hospitality was on full display. I was also shocked at how engaging the participants were regarding issues of slavery, Blacks in the Civil War, and the historical record of their service. I even had opportunities to share with Black families how I found information on my ancestor.

This curious visit would close a vital gap in our family history. I would discover the name of the mystery writer. One of my purchases that day was a book, *Black Confederates* (Barrow, Seagars & Rosenburg). I was casually reading the book in my spare time one day and I finally came to page seventy-four. I couldn't believe my eyes. There was a paragraph making reference to Turner Hall, my ancestor.

> "Turner Hall, II, born October 11, 1842, in North Carolina, often told stories of his servant days in the war. He seldom failed to speak of his having been an orderly for Gen. Robert E. Lee (possibly so, but unverified). He was brought to Hugo, Oklahoma, by Judge Trice from Mississippi in 1906. Hall went to the Diamond Battle Reunion at Gettysburg in 1938 and later appeared on "We, the people" radio show in New York City. Widely respected by all who knew him, he was buried (according to Otis E. Hays, Jr. of Pierce City, Missouri) near Nettleton, Mississippi." (Jay S. Hoar, *The South's Last Boys in Gray*, 18)

Not only did we learn that he was named after his father but we also learned that he was a very traveled man. Pennsylvania, New York City! Turner Hall, Jr. was born a slave in North Carolina in 1840 *(not in Rankin County, North Carolina, as one article suggests; there is no Rankin County in North Carolina*). We believed he died in 1948. His burial place remains unknown. In the buying and selling of slaves, my great-great-grandfather found himself in Mississippi. I am not sure of the transactions that led to his departure from North Carolina. However, we are certain that he must have been separated from his immediate family. Our family history reveals no record that his father, my great-great-great-grandfather, Turner Hall, Sr. ever left North Carolina. In honor of Turner Hall, Sr., from this point forward, I refer to my great-great-grandfather as Turner, Jr. It's a way to remind me that he had a dad whom I'm sure loved him very much.

A young slave boy: Through research, it is revealed to us that at some point in his youth he found himself among the property holdings of one of the most revered Confederate families, "The Family firm of Nathan Bedford Forrest." For the record, the Forrest firm was a very successful and large slave-trading company. After the war, Forrest made huge profits by working ex-slaves in the penal system throughout the South. However, Turner, Jr. was among the former dealings of the Forrest family personal slave plantation, instead of his penal operations. It is believed based upon a 1937 newspaper article that his appreciation for Nathan Bedford Forest was one that would have developed over time. He portrayed a kind of expressed appreciation that a faithful and loyal slave would have had for a faithful master in his day.

Not many African Americans know or even care to know who owned their ancestors. Slavery is a thing of the past and the difficulty of Blacks as property and not as people hinders the efforts that most African Americans would like to take to find out more about their ancestry.

My first introduction to family genealogy came at the expense of my dear wife. It occurred at a family reunion, one of her first gatherings with my family. Thanks to cousin Troy Lee having one too many beers, genealogy became a source of laughter for some time. Cousin Troy Lee, an older relative in the family, saw her getting out of the car and was so struck by her beauty he exclaimed in a full drunken voice, "A full-blooded Choctaw! Come here, babe! I got full-blood Cherokee in my veins!" He picked her up off her feet and gave her a bear hug and a kiss before I could get around the vehicle to save her from her despair. Needless to say, she kept an eye out for ol' Troy Lee for the next two family reunions. I knew my wife wasn't a Choctaw and Troy Lee was the blackest Cherokee I had ever seen if there were any truth to his claim. The fact that we are uniquely referred to as African Americans speaks volumes to the reality that we, Blacks in America, are inherently linked to the motherland, Africa. Indeed, we were brought to this country as slaves. I just happen to be one of those who care enough about that link and all that it represents. I dared to research the depths of what it means to me. I was given a window of opportunity to find out more about my ancestors through this one ancestor, Turner Hall.

A young man—Confederate flunkie: At the start of the Civil War, Turner, Jr. was between nineteen and twenty-one years old. Family research shows he served as a "body servant" for two Confederate soldiers and there is one reference to him as an "orderly" for Robert E. Lee (although unverified). Being a flunky, orderly, or servant for Confederate soldiers was routine duty for many enslaved men of his age. Although it must be known that these men would have fought, if needed.

I am not one that contends that large numbers of slaves were incorporated as soldiers in the Confederacy. I am one to contend that thousands of slaves served the Confederacy in various capacities. Some did serve as soldiers. This fact is evident based upon the pension records and multiple historical accounts that can easily be found with proper research. Both sides of the war were officially reluctant to employ slaves or free Blacks as soldiers. By the end of the war, both sides had changed their minds in this regard. There is nothing in the historical record that we can find that my great-great-grandfather's role as a servant in the Confederate army and orderly for General Lee was ever disputed. He lived during a time when many ex-Confederates lived and not once do we find any dispute of his claim to have served faithfully throughout the war. I think one reason we find no dispute is that his words, like most men of his day, were truthful words. It's certainly hard for a modern man to come to grips with the reality that there once was a time when a man's word was his bond. He did not speak unless he spoke with honor and truth.

As far as his capacity as a flunky or orderly, not much is specifically recorded about the duties of such individuals other than what is commonly known. They did whatever was needed to assist those they served. The fact that many Blacks were written out of the history by writers who took no interest in the roles of Blacks doesn't mean that they didn't have roles. In fact, it is widely known that had it not been for the flunkies, orderlies, and servants who labored for the Confederacy, their fight would have not been as productive as it was in many fronts. The home front of the Southerners alone would have virtually collapsed had it not been for the slaves carrying on their duty. After all, Southern men went to fight while their women and children were left to attend the home front. Fortunately, for some former slaves, verifycation is possible through pension records. Unfortunately, for far too many Black Confederate servants, it is impossible to verify their service to the Confederacy.

What is clear to our family is that Turner Hall, Jr. not only started the war with the Confederacy; he ended the war with the Confederacy and was very proud of it. Moreover, one must ask himself today what were the circumstances that would have led a slave to serve beside Confederate soldiers? All too common is the notion that they served because they had to. Although that may have been the circumstances for some it is not that black and white. Some served because they got paid as cooks and for other tasks in the army. That would have been a tangible way for them to provide for their families. Inflationary costs were extremely high during the Civil War just like in any war. Many had never left their communities or states, and it was unrealistic at that time to venture the risk of life with family that could have included small children or elders. Another circumstance would have been enduring relationships developed between body servants and those they served. Contrary to our modern thought of what we would have done or thought, these people were real people who developed real lasting relationships even across racial lines.

A man (and loyal servant): At the age of twenty-three the war had ended for Turner, Jr. Boys go off to war and they come back men. What of the slave? Was he not subject to the same toils of war, if not worse? His plight was intimately tied to the plight of his masters. From those days in 1861–1865 to this day, bullets and cannon balls with all of their gore have never been known to have eyes. Considering that the Civil War has been one of the bloodiest wars our nation has ever endured, I wonder how many times he was almost killed? Do people really think that Black men were sitting under the shade trees watching White men fight? If so, that's a wrong perception of what actually happened. I can assure you that when the Black men heard the roar of the cannon, he ducked just as the White man beside him. At the same time, when men were called to fight, Black men also took it upon themselves to fight. Again, I do not contend that there was wholesale use of Black men fighting with arms for the Confederacy, or even the Union for that matter. However, the historical record of Blacks during times of war is clear. Black men have had a role in every war in the history of this country dating back to the Revolutionary War.

I cannot devalue the role of Turner, Jr. in the Confederate army. To do so, would be to undermine his character and the character of the thousands of other servants and even Black Confederate soldiers who fought and died during a war that was epic. There has always been a dispute about the value, role, or capacity of Black men's involvement in wars. Even today, in 2015, at the writing of this manuscript, a posthumous award, the highest military award, was given to a Black soldier, Pvt. Henry Johnson, for his bravery in World War I in 1918; an act that was well recorded and known by his superiors but written out of history because of his race. Forgotten! How about the fact that he is just now being remembered ninety-seven years later? I will not forget Turner, Jr. I will remember him and the flag that he honored. One hundred and fifty years later after the war, I will tell his story.

Look at this way. It is only forty-nine years between the end of the Civil War and the start of World War I. That short span of fifty years didn't see much improvement in the equality of African Americans in military ranks. In fact, many African Americans were turned away for military service during World War I despite their willingness and ability to serve. African Americans had proved themselves in the Indian Wars and the Spanish-American Wars. The infamous Buffalo Soldiers were formed just one year after the end of the Civil War in 1866. When you put things in perspective, the proximity of these wars is very close and the continuity of service of African Americans has been consistent throughout history. Thus, I don't have to agree with all that the Confederacy represents in order to hold it in high esteem. I choose to honor my ancestor from a historical perspective and that is the focus of Confederate heritage.

On the other hand, I don't have to tear down the history of the Confederacy or forget it all together. Turner, Jr. didn't do that, and I can't allow the hijacking of the Confederacy in my generation and the previous generation to destroy the historical implications that he shared with many African-American men, though they were slaves at the time. They were men of their time. It is improper to take your existing time span and historical perspective and apply it to the lens of time and history by removing the original historical context. Applying a new historical context to a previous period is simply wrong. Men who used the Confederate flag to portray supremacist views and bigotry brought the flag of the Confederacy back into use during the civil rights era. The battle flag of the Confederate army had not flown since the end of the war in 1865.

I often wonder about the first Confederate soldier that he served. What happened to him? Was he killed? Did he get wounded? If so, did he return home? If so, why and the hell didn't my great-great-grandfather go home with him? He would stay until the end. Was the second Confederate soldier a friend of the first? I can assume they very well could have been boyhood companions of Turner, Jr. That was often the pattern. Because there are virtually no records on slaves in the war at that time, these are questions that perhaps I will never know. Yet, there is one thing I am certain. Turner, Jr. was loyal. Call him what you will; during the war, several terms were used for servants. They were called flunkies, slaves, contraband, body servants, and orderlies. I am OK with these terms. I don't marvel at the terms. He was a man of Confederate conviction and a man with a sense of purpose. And that is what I marvel at. Did he have options? I'm almost certain he did. Perhaps his options weren't as grand as the modern Black man would like to think they would have been. Perhaps he considered choosing to run north or to join the Union. The fact remains, he didn't do either. He finished the course of the war as a Confederate orderly and returned to Mississippi after the war.

A family man: Turner, Jr. married Francis Dilworth on January 12th, 1876. They were married in Monroe County, Mississippi. By this time, he had worked for a prominent family in Okolona, Mississippi, for ten years. He worked for the Walton family in the neighboring county of Chickasaw. From 1879–1898 nine children were born to this union. His last daughter, Willie L. Hall, born March 27, 1898, was my great-grandmother.

Turner, Jr. was a very loyal man. Mr. Walton died and his wife, Mary, married into another prominent family in Okolona. She married Colonel Trice. Turner, Jr. served this Walton family line for four generations. When Mrs. Trice decided to move the family to Oklahoma, Turner, Jr. went with the family. They arrived in Hugo, Oklahoma, in 1906. He would care for one more generation of Waltons in Oklahoma. To this day, we still have relatives spread throughout Oklahoma.

"Aged Negro Serving Fifth In One Line"
Hugo Man Knew Lee in Civil War.

"Hugo, Nov. 24- (Special)- Turner Hall, 95 – at an early age "belonged to the family firm" of Gen. Nathan B. Forrest and Colonel Chambers.

He flunkied for the two Confederates during the Civil war and he saw Gen. Robert E. Lee "lots of times." He still cherishes Confederate money given to him by General Forrest."*(The Daily Oklahoman,* Nov 25, 1937, The Oklahoma Historical Society)

I have secured seven newspaper articles on Turner, Jr. which have become historical artifacts for our family. We received five of these articles from the Oklahoma Historical Society in April of 2015. It was through these discoveries that we came to appreciate not only his loyalty to his Confederate service but his great appreciation for Nathan Bedford Forrest.

How ironic. The timing of the discovery was just two months away from the Charleston South Carolina church shooting that would reignite the battle over the Confederate flag; I was deep into my Confederate history. At least my family would have a historical perspective on the matter of the flag, Nathan Bedford Forrest, and Blacks in the Confederate army.

From the newspaper articles alone, we learned so much about Turner, Jr. He, for his time, was a well-traveled man. To this day, I can't lay claims that I have seen Washington DC or New York City. Since the election of our first African-American president, Washington DC has become the Mecca experience for Black folks. It's not about Washington DC as much as it is seeing Washington DC while Obama is still in office. That's the goal! That is what makes a trip to DC so sweet for many African Americans who have made this journey over the past seven years.

Turner, Jr. was well respected in his community. As a delegate, he received an all-expense-paid trip sponsored by a prominent company and citizens of the town of Hugo. We would come to find out that this would not be his only all-expense-paid trip. We are able to identify three separate trips that the citizens of Hugo gladly paid for him. The articles showed respect for Turner, Jr. was not only from White citizens but from Black citizens, as well. The faithful and loyal servant was now being served.

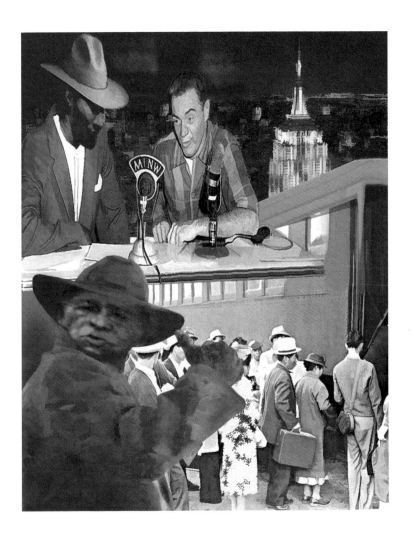

"Hugo's Civil War Veteran and Escort Now In Washington, D.C."

"When 1,000 veterans of the Blue and of the Gray bade one another sad farewells Tuesday and started home from Gettysburg, Pa., Hugo's delegates to the last reunion of Civil War Veterans, Turner Hall, and his escort James H. Milling, entrained for Washington, D.C., to "see the sights." (July 6, 1938 *Hugo Daily News*, Oklahoma Historical Society)

"A Real Pioneer"

"Pictured above is Uncle Turner Hall, colored Civil War veteran, who will soon celebrate his 101st birthday. He will be given a prominent place in the Thursday evening parade and the Cavalcade 1941 shows. During the Civil War, Uncle Turner was an orderly for Robert E. Lee. He has received many honors because of his age and prominence and even appeared on the NBC program, "We, the People" in New York City. The white and colored citizens of Hugo both designate Uncle Turner as their most distinguished citizen." (*Hugo Daily News*, August 28, 1941, Oklahoma Historical Society)

Out of all the articles, there was one that I received by total surprise. This particular article celebrating Turner, Jr.'s hundredth birthday would be the one that brought me to nothing less than an exuberant dance and to tears before my family. I told my daughter to tell her children and her grandchildren the day she saw her daddy dance over the news that he received about his great-great-grandfather. It was Monday, July 20, 2015, in the midst of the turmoil over the Confederate flag following the aftermath of the nine Black Americans killed in an historic church in South Carolina. On this day, I received a final piece of the puzzle of my ancestor's involvement in the Civil War. There were two important components missing about his story. The first, could his claims be verified? I had a third-party written account of his report serving as an orderly for Robert E. Lee in the August 28, 1941, news article (*The Hugo Daily News*). There was also mention in the November 25, 1937, article (*The Daily Oklahoman*) that he saw General Lee "lots of times." But, of course, I had no way of verifying any claims of his service to the Southern General. I had no reason to doubt but, boy, wouldn't it be sweet to actually be able to say for certain that, indeed, it is true!

I was beyond the point of doubting that he was a Confederate. That much was clear. At this point, it was all about historical accuracy to the best of my ability. I had written the Oklahoma Historical Society to request a second copy of the original articles that I had received in April of 2015. I had also obtained his date of birth and inquired about another article that I knew existed but hadn't been delivered in the first search request. It was an article titled "Turner Hall Has Birthday Today, He's 98 Years Old." The article was in the family possession but it was so faded that we could barely read it. In fact, we had to use a magnifying glass to make out the top half of the article and it was almost impossible to read the bottom portion. I knew I needed to get as much information as possible while the getting was good. So, I requested a specific search of this article. This is one of my favorite articles on Turner, Jr.

"Turner Hall Has Birthday Today.
He's 98 Years Old."

"Turner Hall, one of the few surviving Confederate veterans, awoke this morning to find himself 98 years old. When the dawn broke this morning, it was the 35,468th time that daylight had found him still numbered among the living although he went through one of the hardest fought wars in the history of the world.

The venerable colored man, known to almost everybody in Hugo and surrounding towns, does not show his 98 years. In action and appearance he would be taken for a man of 70. He still has a quick eye and a spry step and continues to get around without assistance. He knows on sight almost everyone he meets on the streets.

Last Spring Hall was awarded will all expenses paid to the last meeting of the Blues and Grays at Gettysburg.

Newsreel cameramen singled him out as a typical example of the colored Confederate soldier and depicted him proudly displaying his medals. Hall was an orderly for General Robert E. Lee in the Civil War." (*The Hugo Daily News*, October 11, 1938, Oklahoma Historical Society)

Figure 1 1938 Gettysburg Reunion Program

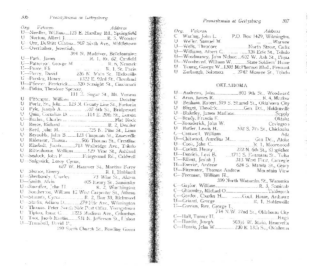

Figure 2 Interior 1938 Gettysburg Reunion Program

This was the third article that we had that made reference to General Robert E. Lee. But this was not the article of surprise that settled my heart and mind on my connection to the Confederacy once and for all. Not only did I receive the ninety-eighth birthday article, a new article emerged during the search since we had narrowed his birthday down to October 11. His hundredth-year birthday celebration made the news in 1940. A familiar large hat with the title, "Has Birthday," and a subtitle, "Turner Hall," helped me put to rest once and for all that I was as much a son of the Confederacy than any Southerner could claim. In fact, one historical aspect in this article settled a personal secret suspicion that I have carried for years. I remembered the words that I read in the book, *Black Confederates*, in Otis Hayes, Jr's account of his conversations with Turner, Jr. in relationship to General Lee as being "unverified." So, for some time, I have been trying to, at a minimum, verify what roles an orderly played in the Civil War. That would be the extent that I would know my ancestor's journey in the war. In fact, this has led me to studying the Civil War with a slave's perspective in mind. Anything that I can find about the Civil War that has accounts of slaves and their role and disposition during the war is of great interest to me.

I had resolved to put the idea of attempting to verify any claims of my great-great-grandfather out of my mind. It would be like trying to find a needle in a haystack. Think about it. How can I verify something that wasn't verifiable? A hundred and fifty years later, how in the world am I to verify any claim that a former slave made when I knew very well that most involvement of slaves in the Civil War were not recorded? It was a helpless plea to say the least. So, you can image my excitement and the reason I danced with joy when I came to the last sentence of this newly discovered article celebrating his hundredth birthday: "His claims to this distinction have been verified from records in the war department." (*The Hugo Daily News*, October 13, 1940, Oklahoma Historical Society)

Any Civil War student will know the significance of this sentence. Verification is everything to those who study the Civil War. The history making of the Civil War, in my opinion, makes it the supreme historical event of our country., so imagine the frustration knowing that your ancestor has claims to history that you know deep down you will never be able to verify. Well, I no longer have that burden. I don't have to verify his claims. Someone else has already done that and that is good enough for me. After all, the accuracy of verification in his day would be more certain than anything I could lay down now. As stated previously, I didn't doubt his claims, because men were truthful men in those days.

There was more. As a student of the Civil War, I have read the accounts many times and often came across references to orderlies performing their duty.

Commonly, no mention of name or even race is given in these accounts. Just "orderly." I'm also aware that an orderly was not necessarily Black; many Whites served in this capacity, and some with greater distinction than others. I could imagine that Robert E. Lee would have had many official military orderlies during the course of the war. So, I had to be careful in my understanding of my ancestor's role as an orderly and how and where he may have been used in various capacities for several individuals.

I did have one verbal witness from Otis Hayes, Jr. to the claim that Turner, Jr. had taken care of Traveller, general Robert E. Lee's horse. (By the way, the first horse owned by my son was named Traveller in honor of his great great-great-grandfather. And this was well before we knew any connection that he had actually claimed to have taken care of one of the most famous war horses of all times.) I could only imagine that an orderly's duty would have been to take care of the horses so that's the hope that I had when my son was fifteen years old and we bought that horse for his birthday in 2009. Moreover, there is a Civil War account that I have read numerous times and wondered if it was remotely possible that my great-great-grandfather could have been there to witness an illustrious Civil War scene. It was at the surrender of General Robert E. Lee to General Grant at Appomattox Courthouse in Virginia on April 9, 1865. The account reads as following:

"At a little before 4 o'clock General Lee shook hands with General Grant, bowed to the other officers, and with Colonel Marshall left the room. One after another we followed, and passed out to the porch. Lee signaled to his orderly to bring up his horse, and while the animal was being bridled the general stood on the lowest step and gazed sadly in the direction of the valley beyond where his army lay— now an army of prisoners. He smote his hands together a number of times in an absent sort of way; seemed not to see the group of Union officers in the yard who rose respectfully at his approach, and appeared unconscious of everything about him. All appreciated the sadness that overwhelmed him, and he had the personal sympathy of everyone who beheld him at this supreme moment of trial. The approach of his horse seemed to recall him from his reverie, and he at once mounted. General Grant now stepped down from the porch, and, moving toward him, saluted him by raising his hat. He was followed in this act of courtesy by all our officer present: Lee raised his hat respectfully, and rode off to break the sad news to the brave fellows whom he had so long commanded." *("Surrender at Appomattox, 1865," EyeWitness to History, www.eyewitnesstohistory.com, 1997)*

What a scene. To be an eye witness to this
account must have been breathtaking. I have read this
account many times wondering about that orderly. I
have held a crazy secret suspicion that perhaps it was
my great-great-grandfather. I am almost certain, based
upon historical records, that this orderly was not my
ancestor, but to have that thought has been a
stimulating aspect of my research.

Yet, hold on. That hundredth birthday article
says records in the war department have verified his
claims. What claims? Well, the article lays out several
claims. One is that he was in the Southern army. I
knew that already. The second claim is that he was an
orderly for Robert E. Lee. I knew about that claim as
well. However, it was a new claim that causes me to
tremble every time I read it. He was at the surrender
of Lee to Grant at Appomattox. Now, that was a
shocker. I don't claim he was the orderly that brought
Traveller to the general on that day. That orderly was
Sergeant Tucker. Tucker was one of the general's
official military orderlies.

I don't claim that my ancestor was an official
military orderly as designated by the Southern army. I
think my ancestor picked that distinction up
throughout the course of the war as he performed
routine servant duties for the general when in his
presence upon numerous occasions. However, I do
believe he was there to witness the surrender of the
Southern army at Appomattox. There is one more

account of orderly servants being at Appomattox. I am inclined to believe that one of these men would have been Turner Hall, Jr. at Appomattox, the Confederates received over 28,000 parole passes. It is recorded that at least thirty-six of these passes were for Blacks. These men were the servants, cooks, and slaves present in various capacities according to the Southern Historical Society Papers. Some of these men are named as teamsters and at least sixteen of them were not named. Again, I don't contend that Turner Hall was a Black Confederate soldier. He was a servant in the Confederate army, and a proud one indeed. He cherished his memories of his time in the war and held dear his association with General Robert E. Lee and Nathan Bedford Forrest. As his great-great grandson, that's enough for me.

Black men took on various roles in the war just as White men did. His service was of no less value in the cause of war and thus must be honored as such. The dilemma of war records creates a problem for Blacks who desire to know the role that their ancestors played in the Southern army, and it presents a current-day problem for the average Confederate ancestor who is aware that slaves were by their ancestors' side. Here is the problem. The record shows that 36 slaves received parole on behalf of the Confederate army of Northern Virginia. However, just because we only have record of 36, it doesn't mean that only 36 were there. What we need to embrace as

African Americans is the fact that we were on the scene. Many of my dear, hard-core Confederates will ask proof of every single detail in the Civil War without ever mentioning the fact that most of the Confederate records burned when the Rebels fled the capitol of Richmond, Virginia. Even had these records been preserved, however, they would be spotty, at best, regarding the history of the Negro. We don't know the full detail of the role Blacks played in the war because we don't have all the records and what was written after the war was almost always a discredit to the Negroes service on both sides. So, those who hold on to Confederate heritage want African Americans to be proud of their ancestors who participated in this heritage without given allowance of what history has done to destroy those con-nections. As a result, there is often little defense or proof with which to overwhelm African Americans as to their Confederate connections. Well, I have found my heritage, and I am proud of it. Not one hard-core Confederate or Black Nationalist will change the fact that my ancestor played a role in the making of this great country:

> "Uncle Turner is a Civil War veteran, having served in the Southern army and was orderly for General Robert E. Lee com-mander of the Southern armies and was present when Gen. Lee surrendered to

General Grant. His memory is excellent and he enjoys relating his experience in connection with his services for the famous Southern general." (*Hugo Daily News*, Oct. 13, 1940, Oklahoma Historical Society).

What started for me in 2008 at a family reunion has climaxed in the middle of the debate on the Confederate flag in 2015. Tears come to my eyes as I realize that my research into my family history has not been in vain. To know that my great-great-grand-father was present at Appomattox at the end of the beginning of a new era for slaves is a humbling fact. That he lived through the war to tell about his story and to lay claims to his Confederate heritage is mind-blowing to me. To be able to write about his story and my journey is an honor. I am intimately tied to the history of our country, the Civil War, and the existing tension between those who struggle to see the Confederate flag remain versus those who struggle to see it come down. I am connected to two of the greatest military generals of all times, Robert E. Lee and Nathan Bedford Forrest, in a strange and twisted way, but in a way that is historic and unique. It would be enough to be connected to one of these great generals. I am connected to two great Confederate generals through Turner Hall, Jr. This gives me the reason to say that I am a two-time Confederate over. That's Southern slang to mean I am twice as much a

Confederate than any other man. I just happen to be Black.

I am fortunate to be able to write about my great-great-grandfather's story. I realize that he was not the only Black slave who served in the Confederacy. Some even fought as soldiers. Opening up one family history with research will lead you down bifurcated roads that have twists and turns that are often unexpected. This is one journey that I am glad I decided to take.

I will forever cherish this story and the role my ancestor played in the Civil War. I pray that it is never forgotten. Unfortunately, because of the brutal injustice imposed upon African Americans by post-Civil War writers, many African Americans can't make any connections to the Civil War. Their connections were destroyed, ignored, hidden, or portrayed with malice. As a result, the heroism of slave Robert Smalls of South Carolina and freeman of color named William Tillman are virtually unknown by African Americans today. Before I share with you the heroism of these two Blacks, let me share a few official military records of some of the service our people conducted in the war in the Confederate army.

To find out what was going on with Blacks during the war, I found it most helpful to find out what Black writers were saying before and during the war. I will refer to the story of Robert Smalls and William Tillman, if nothing more than to stir up a need for African Americans to discover the richness of African-American history that is tied to the Civil War. For those that are not content that my ancestor's role was not as stimulating to them as they would prefer, and because as one of my first cousins said to me at the family reunion, "that's the one who fought on the wrong side?" (I looked at him and said, "That's the one who fought and served!"), I contend that any role in war is a significant role. I think any role in the Civil War has even more special meaning to the establishment of this great nation. But let's look at these two men who surpassed anything that any Union soldier ever accomplished on the high seas of war.

The Story of Robert Smalls, *U.S. Steamship Augusta*, Off Charleston, May 13, 1862:

"Sir, I have the honor to inform you that the rebel-armed gunboat *Planter* was brought out to us this morning from Charleston by eight contrabands (slaves) and delivered up to the squadron. Five colored women and three children are also on board. She was the armed dispatch and transportation steamer attached to the engineer department at Charleston, under Brig.-Gen. Ripley. At four in the morning, in the absence of the captain who was on shore, she left her wharf close to the government office and headquarters, with the Palmetto and Confederate flags flying, and passed the successive forts, saluting as usual, by blowing the steam-whistle. After getting beyond the range of the last gun, they hauled down the rebel flags, and hoisted a white one. *The Onward* was the inside ship of the blockading squadron in the main channel, and was preparing to fire when her commander made out the white flag.

"The armament of the steamer is a thirty-two pounder, on pivot, and a fine twenty-four pound howitzer. She has, besides, on her deck, four other guns, one seven-inch, rifled, which were to be taken on the following morning to a new fort on the middle ground. One of the four belonged to Fort Sumter, and had been struck, in the rebel attack, on the muzzle. Robert Small, the intelligent slave, and pilot of the boat, who performed this bold feat so skillfully, is a superior man to any who have come into our lines, intelligent as any of them have been. His information has been most interesting, and portions of it of the utmost importance. The steamer is quite a valuable acquisition to the squadron by her good machinery and very light draught. The bringing out of this steamer would have done credit to anyone. I do not know whether, in the view of the Government, the vessel will be considered a prize; but if so, I respectfully submit to the Department the claims of the man Small and his associates. Very respectfully, your obedient servant, S. F. DuPont, "Flag-Officer Commanding."

Commercial Advertiser said:

"We are forced to confess that this is a heroic act, and that the Negroes deserve great praise. Small is a middle-aged Negro, and his features betray nothing of the firmness of character he displayed. He is said to be one of the most skillful pilots of Charleston, and to have a thorough knowledge of all the ports and inlets of South Carolina." (William Wells Brown, *The Negro in The American Rebellion*, 1867)

"*The Planter* is just such a vessel as is needed to navigate the shallow waters between Hilton Head and the adjacent islands, and will prove almost invaluable to the Government. It is proposed, I hear, by the commodore, to recommend the appropriation of $20,000.00 as a reward to the plucky Africans who have distinguished themselves by this gallant service, $5,000 to be given to the pilot, and the remainder to be divided among his companions. (William Wells Brown, *The Negro in The American Rebellion*,1867)

The Story of William Tillman:

"In the month of June, 1861, the schooner *S. J. Waring*, from New York, bound to South America, was captured on the passage by the rebel privateer *Jeff Davis*, a prize crew put on board, consisting of a captain, mate and four seamen; and the vessel set sail for the port of Charleston, SC. Three of the original crew was retained on board, a German as steersman, a Yankee who was put in irons, and a black man named William Tillman, the steward and cook of the schooner. The latter was put to work at his usual business and told that he was henceforth the property of the Confederate States, and would be sold, on his arrival at Charleston, as a slave. Night comes on; darkness covers the sea, the vessel is gladdening swiftly toward the South; the rebels, one after another, retire to their berths; the hour of midnight approaches; all is silent in the cabin; the captain is asleep; the mate, who has charge of the watch, takes his brandy toddy, and reclines upon the quarter-deck. The Negro thinks of home and all its endearments; he sees in the dim future chains and slavery.

He resolves, and determines to put the resolution into practice upon the instant. Armed with a heavy club, he proceeds to the captain's room. He strikes the fatal blow: he feels the pulse, and all is still. He next goes to the adjoining room: another blow is struck, and the black man is master of the cabin. Cautiously he ascends to the deck, strikes the mate: the officer is wounded but not killed. He draws his revolver, and calls for help. The crew are aroused: they are hastening to aid their commander. The Negro repeats his blows with the heavy club: the rebel falls dead at Tillman's feet. The African seizes the revolver, drives the crew below deck, orders the release of the Yankee, puts the enemy in irons, and proclaims himself master of the vessel. *The Waring's* head is turned toward New York, with the stars and stripes flying, a fair wind, and she rapidly retraces her steps. A storm comes up: more men are needed to work the ship. Tillman orders the rebels to be unchained and brought on deck. The command is obeyed; and they are put to work, but informed, that, if they show any disobedience, they will be shot down. Five days more, and the *The S. J. Waring* arrives in the port of New York, under the command of William Tillman, the Negro patriot."

The *New York Tribune* said of this event:

"To this colored man was the nation indebted for the first vindication of its honor on the sea." The Federal Government awarded to Tillman the sum of six thousand dollars as prize-money for the capture of the schooner. (William Wells Brown, *The Negro in The American Rebellion*, 1867)

Here are the stories of Black Civil War-era men. They had no formal education, no right to vote, no opportunity for advancement, no right to military service. These were mere men who were faced with obstacles beyond imagination for the average African-American man today.

They were slaves and some were free in a country that had condoned slavery for four hundred years. They all survived, though, through very different means. My ancestor used chivalry and service as a slave. The other man overcame with ingenuity and intelligence. Finally, one overcame with a club and a revolver. One man fought and served under the Confederate flag. Two men fought under the American flag. Which flag represented a system of oppression and slavery from the perspective of the African?

We forget that slavery existed for years under the American flag. The Confederate flag came during the last four years of slavery. The greatest tragedy is that as African Americans we don't know these stories, and yet, we disown the men of this era as if they were mere pawns in a game of chess. These men fought, served, and lived during a time that was the beginning of a new formation for our country. They were more than pioneers. As much as I want to say that they were the foundations in which African-American men are built upon today, I am too embarrassed to say that. It appears that they are more like capstones or the apex of what it means to be African-American men. I say this because, if these men had the odds that the average African-American male had today, they would walk among us as giants. Why? It is because these men and women overcame unbelievable obstacles. They could not read or write but they could navigate ships on the high seas, they could command ships and navigate waters. They were slaves, but they weren't afraid to master the trade of their day in order to accomplish great heights. They could traverse land or sea, and discharge their duties with complete competence.

This is why I write of the need for Black guilt instead of White guilt. When I think of men like these, I hang my head every time I see a young Black man arrested for senseless acts of violence and crime that plague our communities; when I witness the degradation of the Black family into a cycle of poverty because men will not take their rightful place as men and be respectful citizens of our society and raise their children to be respectful citizens in a free country. Martin Luther King, Jr. said, "Freedom has always been expensive." Why are so many of our men incarcerated? Too few seek to serve our country through military service when opportunities are enormous before them. On the eve of the emancipation proclamation in 1863, slave George Payne explained freedom this way:

> "Let me tell you, though, don't be too free! De lazy man can't go to heaven. You must be honest, an' work, an' show

dat you is fit to be free; an' de lord will bless you an' Abrum Lincum. Amen!" (George Payne, Slave 1863, William Wells Brown, *The Negro in The American Rebellion*)

Turner Hall was a hard worker. He didn't just work for the Walton family for five generations. When he arrived in Oklahoma, the first thing he did was help the Walton's build their family home. He then built his own personal cabin behind their home and it became a "landmark for many years." He was a janitor for the First Baptist church for fifteen years. He was janitor of the Ross building for thirteen years and the First Presbyterian Church for nearly ten years. If there is any man in our family who does not work, we will be the first to say, he doesn't deserve to eat. That doesn't mean we don't feed the hungry or the poor. It simply means we place a very high value on hard work. There was never a day that a stranger couldn't get a meal at my grandmother's home. She cooked for her family and always prepared enough for the straggler that would come to her house with her grandchildren or her kids. The descendants of Turner Hall, Jr. are hard workers. My dad and his siblings, to this day, are very hard workers. They made their living by the sweat of their brow. They worked their way up from the bottom of manufacturing, military service, and education to the top of the workforce. They have all done well by the grace of God and by working hard and demonstrating their ability to be dependable workers.

My dad was plant manager for Mid-South Packing Company in Tupelo. I remember seeing him get off work when I was a young man. All supervisors wore white hats on his job. His hat was red. The buck stopped with him. I was always proud of him knowing that he was at the top of his industry without a formal education.

Uncle Willie retired from manufacturing and started his own manufacturing company. He was very successful and retired a second time from his work.

Currently, my brother, Kenny Hill, is the owner and operator of this company, with my dad right by his side. Uncle Willie still has one eye on everything that goes on.

Aunt Pearl retired in education as an administrator and school principal in Michigan schools, being the only college graduate (Michigan State, Administration) in the family.

Aunt Avis is the manager of Alan White's Furniture in Shannon, Mississippi.

Uncle Ralph retired from the Air Force and continues to work in his industry as an expert in aviation mechanics.

Uncle Earnest, a Vietnam Veteran, retired as a plant manager from manufacturing in Grand Rapids, Michigan.

Uncle Herbert, a laborer, was the president of the Union Association for Eljer's Manufacturing in Tupelo and traveled throughout the United States and Canada on his job.

They all got their hard work ethics from their parents who got it from their parents, who got it from their parents. One of my grandfather's favorite saying was, "If you are going to be a ditch digger, be the best ditch digger you can be." Ras Arnold was an un-educated man who learned to master electrical work and plumbing.

My grandmother, Arine Arnold, was "The Help" for the prominent Black family (owners of Black's Clothing Store) in Nettleton. To say that "Moma Arine" and Mrs. Black were anything short of best friends for life would be an understatement. These two friends were inseparable in life. They are truly no longer separated by race, class, or which side of town they lived own. They are now united as one in the same heaven that awaits all who put their trust in Christ. Just like her grandfather, Turner Hall, Jr. who found a friend and brother in Nathan Bedford Forrest, their friendship was built upon a relationship that spanned over forty years. I'm certain that relationship had its ups and downs. But they persevered accepting the same Christ as their Redeemer.

It saddens me today as I see the numerous and unlimited opportunities for educational experiences that are never tapped into because far too many of our young men and women want an easy way to success. Hard work is no longer the way for too many.

Thank you, Billy Yank!

Health Worker Is Hugo Lions Speaker

HUGO, Okla. (Special).—Ralph Lee, employed by the state health department was a guest of the Hugo Lions Club here Wednesday noon at the Webb Hotel and gave instructions on mosquito and malarial control.

Dr. H. V. Posey, Durant, and Charlie House, Dallas, were also guests. "Uncle" Turner Hall, 98-year-old Negro ex-slave, appeared before the club. He has been selected to appear on "We the People" program in New York City on April 16. Lion members contributed money to aid him in making the trip.

Figure 3The Paris News Thursday April 4, 1940

After my first book, I had a good Yankee friend who wanted to help me prove that I was wrong about my ancestor. So, he took up my story to study it for him-self in an effort to disprove the accounts.

After several weeks, Billy Yank called me and said he had found two more articles on my ancestor and was waving his flag of surrender. He offered to give me the articles if I wanted them. Of course, I didn't refuse the information. I am grateful because one of these articles confirmed the family story that Pappa Turner was returned to Mississippi for burial.

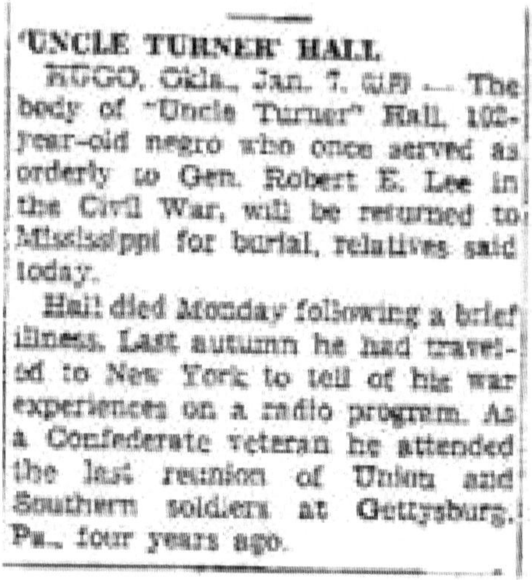

'UNCLE TURNER' HALL

HUGO, Okla., Jan. 7. (AP) — The body of "Uncle Turner" Hall, 102-year-old negro who once served as orderly to Gen. Robert E. Lee in the Civil War, will be returned to Mississippi for burial, relatives said today.

Hall died Monday following a brief illness. Last autumn he had traveled to New York to tell of his war experiences on a radio program. As a Confederate veteran he attended the last reunion of Union and Southern soldiers at Gettysburg, Pa., four years ago.

Figure 4
Amarillo Daily News
Thursday January 8, 1942

This article is the only document that we have regarding the nature of his death. The second article delivered by my newfound Yankee friend was a discovery of my ancestor hanging out at a big-time hotel with some big wigs on his way to New York City.

Am I My Brother's Keeper?

Now Cain said to his brother Abel, "Let's go out to the field."

While they were in the field, Cain attacked his brother Abel and killed him. Then the LORD said to Cain, "Where is your brother Abel?"

"I don't know," he replied. "Am I my brother's keeper?"

The LORD said, "What have you done? Listen! Your brother's blood cries out to me from the ground." (Gen. 4:8–10)

A modern version of the "Am I my brother's keeper?" question came as a result of the 1992 Rodney King riots in Los Angeles. At a post-riot news conference, King coined the question of my generation when he asked, "Can't we all just get along?"

I have come to understand, in very meaningful ways, that without Christ, it is impossible to do two things. First, it is impossible to be your brother's keeper. It doesn't matter if he is White or Black. Secondly, it is impossible for all of us to get along. Humanity is broken. That brokenness shows up in our hatred of one another, our bitterness toward each other, and our unforgiving spirits toward one another. Therefore, the answer to both questions is a resounding NO! We live in a society where we are NOT our brothers' keepers. I want to answer the question emphatically, absolutely not. We can't just all get along! There will always be something that comes up to remind us of our past and provide splinters to wounds. Unless you have reconciled your past and/or your wounds through the blood of Christ, you are doomed to a life of bitterness, unforgiveness, and hatred.

Being that I am African American, let me share with you how this is too often displayed in our communities. When I was in physical therapy school, I rented an apartment from a very successful African-American lawyer in Jackson. He would visit the apartment routinely to monitor the upkeep. I had a picture that portrayed a Black arm stretching over a mountain reaching for another Black arm. This art had been a centerpiece of my living area since my days at Jackson State University. It was a defining principle that I lived by. It was a portrait of one brother helping another brother to overcome mountaintops. Well, I wasn't ready for the perspective of my landlord. He introduced me to a concept that I had never heard of. He asked me, "Young man, have up ever heard the story of a crab in a bucket?"

I replied, "No."

Well, most Black Southerners know exactly where this is going. But, let me tell the rest of you one of the hidden painful secrets among Blacks. This is very painful for the most part. Black folk will talk about this among themselves but we don't prefer to air our dirty laundry to other folks. This particular issue is a troublesome one to the soul of the African American. Moreover, we all have our different reasons as to why and how this is our narrative. This issue has deep roots in our communities and this was my introduction to it. However, it would be years later before I would come face to face with the reality of this. Be it known that I rejected every notion of this mentality upon my introduction. I distinctly remember the pride in which this well-known Black professional gave me his thoughts about my art. He smiled as he told me there was something in the picture that I could not see.

I looked again as I had stared at this picture a few times. He then pointed to the picture and said, "As soon as you grab that hand to lift him up he will pull out a razor and cut your wrist as you pull him up."

We debated this for over an hour. He left me with these words, "You keep living and you will find out!"

I never forgot this exchange. It would stay with me throughout the remainder of my time in physical therapy school.

I graduated from the Physical Therapy school at the University of Mississippi in 1991. One year after graduation, I began my mountaintop reaching experience. I volunteered once a month at Jackson State University, mentoring college students as they pursued their goal to become a physical therapist. After the second year, I added Tougaloo College. For four years, I reached over the mountain to pull others up over the hills. At the end of the four years I started to see a trend that caused me to redirect my energy. First, I saw a rapid decline in the students' desire to succeed. More and more students were farther and farther down the mountain. They were harder to reach because they had not adequately prepared themselves. They were showing up at the foot of the mountain too late and without the tools necessary for the climb. Secondly, I noticed a trend of former mountain climbers turning their hand away from those that were seeking their help. Those that had succeeded would do little, if anything, to help others climb. Frequently, I would receive calls from former students giving me information on some poor student who was a family member or son of a friend that needed help to climb the mountain of becoming a physical therapist. It became clear to me that everyone would not reach back. These were therapists who were now employed with great incomes but were passing students off as if they had the plague.

This was just the beginning of my crab bucket experience. I had not been cut yet but the bucket would soon be full as I started my own private practice in a predominately African-American city. Moreover, a very highly skilled Black professional community existed. Ten years later, I wanted to go back and shake the hand of my former landlord. Unfortunately, he had suddenly died and I was never able to tell him that I had come to experience and know the pain of being in the bucket with a lot of crabs. Brutal is an understatement. All the years of preparation to combat the enemy, and the enemy wasn't who I thought he was. I found out that my biggest enemy looked just like me. He certainly wasn't a blue-eyed devil. In fact, when I sold my company, the blue-eyed physician was my biggest referral source and had it not been for him I wouldn't have been able to feed my family. I received referrals from many White physicians that I never laid eyes on. On the other hand, the unbelievable life experience of working with African Americans was eye opening to say the least.

My Crab Experiences

The Greedy Doctor

I owned the first Black independent physical therapy clinic in the capitol city. Jackson is a Black professional haven, if you will. A large majority of Mississippi's Black professionals practice in the Jackson metropolitan area. When I was in physical therapy school at the University of Mississippi, I served as the vice president of the Minority Student Affairs club. The president of the organization was a medical student that shared a similar story as mine. Most, if not all of us, in the group were first generational college students or from impoverished upbringings. After graduation, I developed a professional relationship with this physician. She referred patients and I provided care accordingly. About two years into the relationship, her referrals stopped. I visited her after I discovered she had started doing physical therapy in a non-conventional way for her patients. I strongly suggested to her that this was not a viable solution for her patients and for her well-being. She had been introduced to a concept of referring patients to herself. Sadly, several years after she refused to listen to the direct ethical challenges of doing what was right and good for the well-being of her patients (overwhelmingly Black), she faced over a hundred years of incarceration for Medicare fraud. Sadly, a common theme in the African-American community was, "They're doing it to her because she is Black." However, records in court showed she had billed millions of dollars. No, it wasn't because she was Black. It was because she was stealing. There was no reason for me to wonder why she stopped referring patients to me. She received a multi-year prison sentence.

The Hit Man from Chicago

This crab experience is perhaps the funniest of all them but it happened. I had two offices at the time. I owned one in Jackson and one in a little small town outside of the Jackson metro area. There was a group of Black physicians who operated a clinic and provided referrals for physical therapy to my clinic. I received a call to set up a meeting with one of the physicians whose practice did not warrant any referrals to my office. I thought the request was strange but it was granted being that he did not refer patients to me. Upon arrival to my office, I noticed the physician was not alone. He had with him an African-American gentleman of great stature. He must have been six foot three inches, with very broad shoulders. He was wearing a pinstripe suit with snakeskin shoes. Church ground clean. This brother was sharp. The physician introduced him as their new office manager that would oversee all out-sourced referrals. He stated to my partner and me, "I understand that we send you over 90 percent of your referrals and if you guys don't come in under us, we are going to pull the plug on you. We are going to go in-house with everything."

Wow! This guy didn't have a gun to my head but I had watched enough movies to know a shake down when I saw one. But the fact that he had the pinstripe suit and the snakeskin shoes made it all surreal to me. I was looking at a real live mobster type figure attempting to shake me down as if I was some punk on the street. And the white-coat bosses that sent this guy were Black guys who I had worked with for years in a small community with a large African-American population. A community that was instrumental in the civil rights era. This group hired a White therapist to work in their office. Within six months, the therapist had resigned and that was the end of their attempt to "go in-house." I never got another referral from them.

The NAACP Front

One of the first invites I got in the local community was an invitation from the local NAACP president who was also a physician. He was a pioneer in the community in some regards. Blacks marched to secure hospital privileges for this physician back in the '60s. Proverbs 27:6 is one of my favorites and it helped me tremendously in this instance. It reads, "the wound of a friend can be trusted but an enemy multiplies kisses."

I remember the day I saw it coming as clearly as if it was this day. The physician's office manager came to my office to "visit your facilities." With a smile as big as Chester the cat himself, she proceeded to walk the building to inspect all of my equipment. I then realized that this guy had sent a spy to my office to see what he needed to provide physical therapy in his office. At that moment, I began to show her everything that I had and how it worked. After all, if they were going to take care of my people, I wanted them to know what they needed. The entire time this lady was smiling and telling how much they appreciated me taking care of their patients. Yet, I could feel her deceit. It was so thick I could cut a cake with it. They hired a White therapist and stopped referring business to me the following week. The therapist resigned after three months and that was the end of that. I never got another referral from my NAACP friend.

The Black Hospital

A small hospital in rural Mississippi was in need of physical therapy services. An all-Black board, a Black CEO, and a Black CFO governed this particular hospital. For two years we courted the CEO and CFO to allow us to establish a contract with the hospital to provide services to the community. After failed attempts to convince them of this direction we decided to open a freestanding clinic in the com-munity. At the direction of the primary Black physician in the com-munity we gave one last attempt to secure a contract with the hospital prior to proceeding with the free standing clinic. Another two weeks expired and the administrator finally agreed to present our contract after two years and two weeks. The boards' attorney was a White guy whose wife was a physical therapist. Need I say more? She got the contract in two weeks and that was that. When I pushed the CFO to explain their decision, her answer was this, "Well, we have a Black board and if we present anything to them that's Black, they will not approve it." Ouch!

The Largest Crab Emerges

During the election of our first Black president, Barack Obama, we witnessed this crab experience on a national level. While most African Americans were elated at the possibility of electing the first African-American president, we witnessed a most em-barrassing but all-too-familiar problem. An unlikely source but not surprising was the old crab claw given by none other than the Rev. Jessie Jackson when he desired to have Barrack Obama castrated for "talking down to Black folks," as he put it. At that time, I realized again that my former landlord had shared something with me that I would never understand but would often see throughout my adult experiences. It's one thing to disagree with a man but to desire him castrated is to signify your desire to see him destroyed.

As an African-American male, one of the biggest disappointments that I have had over the past eight years in the Obama administration is to witness the failure as a community to stop violent crimes among young African-American men. Notice, I did not say, "Obama's failure." However, you would think with the election of our first African-American president, the young African-American males would be inspired to greatness, instead of violence. Let me be clear, the president is not to blame. I have surely felt a lack of outcry from our community in this regard. Where is the marching and protests over the thousand lives claimed in Chicago from January to June 2015? During the same time that Blacks were protesting over the death of Travon Martin, Eric Garner, Michael Brown, and Freddie Grey, thousands of African-American men were being slaughtered at the hands of other African Americans.

This is in not to diminish the spotlight on what African Americans perceive as injustice in the criminal justice system. As Christians, we all are to fight injustice. This is simply to cast a broader light on a much larger problem and the lack of response from the African-American community. Where is the national outcry?

Many have attempted to curtail the violence. But I'm not talking about curtailing it or slowing it down. I'm talking about demanding that it stop with just as much passion as we demand justice for those killed by injustice. Let's attack Black homicides and the senseless crimes in our communities like we attack the Confederate flag and the cases of injustice that we are quickly to rally support for.

Where are the loudmouth preachers, politicians, and movie stars when our communities and heritage are being betrayed by savage acts of violence and hatred toward one another? We have communities that suffer from chronic failure to uphold common decency for our elders, respect for our women, and wholesale disregard for the welfare of children. How long will it take to realize that White folks today or one hundred and fifty years ago are not our problem? We are our worst enemy. We are not our brother's keeper and it is showing up everywhere in our communities.

If our young men are not dying in the streets like dogs they are being locked up in prisons, herded like cattle. In fact, dogs and cattle get more respect in society than the average Black male, thus the movement, Black Lives Matter. If Black lives matter, why are we wholesale murdering each other in the streets? I'll tell you why. Because we want Black lives to matter only when we want them to matter. This ought not be, but we have allowed it. Young men are fathering multiple children by different women, condemning multiple generations to poverty. And what do we say? We parade these facts through lyrics in our most popular songs. "It's just my baby daddy!"

Moreover, thousands upon thousands fail to seize the opportunity to be educated and therefore are not useful for the workforce and not prepared for military service. I see this daily in my line of work as a home health physical therapist. I see first- hand the degradation of the family and the impact that it's having on our people. Hopelessness and despair due to lack of education, lack of skills, poor work ethics, and lack of faith runs through our communities like a plague. Crime is high, abortion rates are skyrocketing, and military readiness is down. The productivity of young African-American males is staggeringly low.

In the backdrop of all of this, many of us want White folks to feel guilty for the crimes of their ancestors and the existing hatred of a few toward Black folks. Even if there is a reason to be guilty, and I contend it no longer exists, the biggest guilt should be on our shoulders. What we need NOW is Black guilt, not White guilt!

After all, it was our people who endured slavery, endured post-Civil Wartime, and endured the Civil Rights era. It was our people who died, sacrificed, and worked like dogs that we may have a better future. It was our people that sacrificed that one day we could see a brother be elected as president of the United States of America. One of my favorite

Martin Luther King, Jr. quotes is, "Freedom has always been an expensive thing." At the expense of four million slaves and at the expense of generations of suffering and sacrifice, we squander opportunities, waste talent, and fail to cultivate family, faith, and respect. We won't even go vote. It took us over a hundred years of persecution to earn the freedom to vote.

It is clear to me that slavery was, to this day, the greatest failure of the implied command to be our brother's keeper. I think the second greatest failure is the holocaust that killed millions of Jews. What makes slavery worse is that it was an institution that occurred over a four hundred-year period of time. What's even more mind boggling about this greatest offense of the implied law of God to be our brother's keeper is that it was other Africans selling their brothers into slavery. Moreover, you can also find records of free Africans in America who owned slaves themselves. A prominent African American in Vicksburg, Mississippi, Robert Johnson, owned twelve slaves at the time of his death. He even had slave quarters behind his home, which can still be viewed as a national registered landmark.

However, I think the biggest violation of the "brother's keeper" concept is among African-American males who commit wholesale homicide and perpetuate fatherless children in our communities. Slavery, race, racism, being African American, civil rights, White heritage, and a post-racial America are all complex things. They are not black and white, as many of us want them to be. The Rodney King riots in Los Angeles, California, brought forth the same question that Cain asked God. King asked the question of the decade, if not the century, "Can't we all just get along?" Again, the answer to that question is a resounding NO! I believe mankind is incapable of this great moral challenge without the intervention of a great moral Guide. Hatred has been in our hearts from the point of original sin until this day. Cain's killing of his brother Abel was indeed the first act of racial discrimination, bias, profiling, murder, jealousy, strife, contention, and blame. We are humanly incapable of getting along. Mankind and his strife have occurred since the beginning of times. It shouldn't be a mystery to us why Cain's question, "Am I my brother's keeper?" is not at the end of the Holy Scriptures but in the beginning.

A primary standard of Christianity starts at what I call "the keeper's point." This is the moment in time that each man succumbs to the interest of others and not just the interest of himself. I don't have to be a keeper of my Confederate brother's culture or heritage but I can learn to value it and honor it as an intricate reality of who I am in Christ. I believe God has helped me understand a fundamental truth of the Gospel. It is this: Those who differ the most from you are the ones you need to love the most. I don't believe it is possible to acquiesce this kind of love without redemption in Christ. This is the reason man is full of hatred, sin, bitterness, and strife. I have a sweet acceptance of who I am and who others are only because of Christ.

History Lessons in Black and White

History Lessons in Black and White are writings that occurred after my first book. They are a collection of the most favorite Facebook Posts that people all over the world has told me of their enjoyment. These posts have reached thousands of people and have stimulated great conversations about race, heritage and relationships. The top post, "Boy, That Flags Is Ours" reached over 125,000 people and brought over 12,000 responses. Enjoy!

Black Confederate Dr's Day!
March 15th
Happy Birthday to Black Confederate, Dick Gray
Better known as Dr. Richard Henry Boyd!!

I will never forget the day I got my distinction of "Dr." in the Great State of Tennessee. To this day, I am known as Dr. Arnold in Tennessee alone. The story behind my distinction is hilarious. Although, there was a real Black Confederate Dr. in Tennessee that is worthy to remember. It was about a year ago that I shared my story on Facebook (March 4, 2016). Facebook, with its memory lane moments, reminded me of one of the funniest things that happened to me since I embraced my Black Confederate Heritage.

At the same time, this Facebook memory reminded me of one of the most painful ironies of my Confederate journey, being uninvited by a Black Missionary Baptist Church during Black History Month, 2016. Not only were my children born in this Church, I had many friends still members of this congregation. One of those friends had enough nerve to recommend my book and me to the Annual Black Family Heritage Event. The committee, without reading the book, invited me to be their guest speaker. Man, I was pumped. You will have to find that post on my page to find out exactly how I was uninvited.

Nevertheless, my focus here is on my Black Confederate Dr's Day Celebration. A former Mississippi Confederate Body Servant, Dick Gray, founded the National Baptist Convention of America. This Convention is the second largest group of African American Christians in America. It has 3.5 million members and over 8,000 churches.

Here is Dick's story. He was born a slave on a plantation in Noxubee County, MS on March 15th, 1843. Dick went to war with his master and three sons. His master, B.W. Gray and two eldest sons were killed in the war. A third son was badly wounded and Dick brought the wounded son home to Texas. Dick assumed all management responsibilities of the Texas plantation and operated it successfully until emancipation. Once free, Dick changed his name to Richard Henry Boyd. A self taught man, learning his alphabets at the age of 22, Dick was committed to the Gospel and to church planting soon after being baptized in a Texas Baptist Church. He is known to have hired a White girl to teach him to read and write. He then enrolled in Bishop College and attended there for two years.

In 1893 Dick formed the General Missionary Baptist Convention of Texas. He went on to be the first to publish Sunday School Materials for Black Baptists. He would join the National Baptist Convention, USA, moving to Nashville, TN after differences with the Texas Convention. He established and personally financed the National Baptist Publishing Board in 1896 as part of the National Baptist Convention, USA. The White Southern Baptist Convention had its main Publishing operations in Nashville and helped Dick publish his materials for Black Sunday Schools. By 1906, Dick had established the largest African American Publishing Company in the country. Of course, this success led to accusations by the National Baptist Convention, USA and brought on a lawsuit in which Dick won, holding on to his Publishing Board.

Dr. Boyd is remembered for being the first to preserve the music of slaves in his work "Plantation Melody Songs" and through his publications of slave songs through the Publishing Board he founded. In 2009, he was awarded (posthumously) induction into the Music City Walk of Fame in Nashville for this contribution to society. An author of more than fourteen works, Dr. Boyd was awarded real honorary doctorate degrees by Alabama A & M College and Guadeloupe University. Now, here is a real Black Confederate Dr.!! Happy Birthday Sir! This story certainly turns history on its head. And those good ol' Black Baptists Well, they've been fighting from the beginning!

A Black Slave Owner, A Black Union Hero and The Louisiana Black History Hall of Fame Twist. Gumbo indeed!

One of the joys I have had in writing the book *Robert E. Lee's Orderly A Modern Black Man's Confederate Journey* is studying Black history that is outside the normal boundaries of traditional Black history. This means that I had to be open to narratives that didn't fit the norm of my formal education. For example, in

1990 the first African America of... Treasurer for Louisiana was inducted to the LA Black History Hall of Fame. Antoine Dubuclet (1810-1887), a prominent free Black who owned up to 100 slaves is a celebrated part of Louisiana Black History. Dubuclet was among the elite groups of free blacks who owned slaves in pre-Civil War Louisiana. He operated one of the largest sugar plantations in Louisiana. Not only did Dubuclet, a Black man, hold office from 1868 to 1878, he was the only person to hold office after the "Battle of Liberty Place" that occurred in 1874 and therefore is connected to the contentious history regarding the removal of monuments at Lee Circle in New Orleans.

In the same New Orleans Cemetery (No. 2) where Dubuclet is buried is another Black Civil War Black history hero, Andre Callioux (1825-1863). A Union Soldier, Callioux was one of the first African American Union soldiers killed in the Civil War during the battle to take Fort Hudson. According to some, his reputation as a patriot and martyr long outlived him. In an 1890 collection of interviews, Civil War Veteran Colonel Douglass Wilson said, "If ever patriotic heroism deserved to be honored in stately marble or in brass that of Captain Callioux deserves to be, and the American people will have never redeemed their gratitude to genuine patriotism until that debt is paid."

In 1860, both of these men were in the same circle of the "Free men of Color" society of New

Orleans that reached a height of 10,000 members just before the war. They both rest in the same New Orleans Cemetery today. But only one is in the Louisiana Black History Hall of fame, the Slave owner, Dubuclet. I wonder what would mayor Mitch Landrieu say to that? Hum!! "West Africa = The Word Okra or Ki nigombo!!!"

Thus, Civil War History is Black History. If you remove ANY Civil War monuments, you will destroy a missing and untold Black History that we are yet to discover. Leave Lee Circle alone or you will be digging up the Cemetery next!!

Boy, That Flag is ours!

Breaking News: So, what does the second oldest living kin to Black Confederate, Turner Hall, Jr. say about the Confederate Flag? At 93 years old, Florine Hall, still living, was married to the grandson of Turner Hall, Jr., Mr. B. Turner Hall (named after his grandfather). When asked this week what she thought about the Confederate Flag, my cousin and her son, Robert E. Hall reports she said, "That Flag is as much ours as it is theirs!"

My cousin heard me speak for the first time on our Black Confederate Heritage and his great grandfather, Turner Hall, Jr. He purchased the book and goes home to share it with his 93 year old mother and this is what he gets. A truth that he did not expect!

"Boy, that's our Flag." Lol!!! He then tells me he went to the Hall's family reunion and it seems like everybody there was name Robert E. Just proof that Black Heritage and Confederate Heritage are one in the same. We are uniquely connected to one another through our Southern roots. (It was after this conversation that I realized Papa Turner had named his first son, Robert and that name continues until this day).

The Day My Black Confederate Heritage Got Me In The White House

Orderlyforlee goes to Washington. Wow! This has been a joy!! In my first book, I wrote that it was every Black man's dream to make it to the White House before President Obama gets out of office. I did not know that that sentence would register in the heart of a guy living in Tippah County Mississippi. I received an email asking me if I wanted to take a trip to the White House and have a personal tour? At first glance, I thought it was a joke. But the more the guy talked the more I was convinced he was telling me the truth; he had a cousin in the White House. So, I came home and told my wife, "My Black Confederate Heritage is going to get us a tour at the White House." She said, "Right" and cast off the thought as it if it were a winter breeze in the middle of summer. When I bought the plane tickets she then said, "Really!"

My newly found Confederate brother, Robert Jackson, from Ripley, Mississippi had a cousin, Dr. Ronny Jackson. Dr. Jackson is the President's Physician. I never told my wife or my new friend, Robert, that I had doubts all the way up until the last minute. I didn't believe until I had a sign from Heaven. When we got to the White House gate and were greeted by a solid black squirrel. At that moment, I had a great Southern sign of hope that we would actually get in and we did. An avid squirrel hunter, that black squirrel received my full presidential pardon on this day. My shotgun will never bear witness to another one of those graceful creatures again. Dr. Jackson gave us a tour through the West Wing, East Wing, Rose Garden and we even saw the President standing in the Oval Office. It was beautiful!!

My wife and I actually got more than we could bargain for. We were celebrating twenty-five years of Marriage and this was my gift to my wife for tolerating me all of those years. I considered this to be a previous, gift to us from our great-great grandfather and Robert E. Lee's Orderly, Turner Hall, Jr. I would have never guessed in a thousand years that my Confederate Heritage would have given me such a personal journey of the most famous house in the world. We saw the China room displaying personal Chinaware by all of our former presidents. We saw every photo of the First Ladies. We stood in the pressroom where the President stands. We also met Mrs. Obama's Physician.

We even trumped where Trump is going to trump! Need I say, this was a special treat and a great 25th wedding celebration.

And yes, the President's physician delivered a copy of my little book, *Robert E. Lee's Orderly*, to the President with personal greetings and love from the great State of Mississippi.

Trump Is Right! Many Sides

Here is why I think President Donald John Trump is right to call out "Many Sides." He reminded me of another time that a violent mob got together to kill a women who had been found guilty of adultery. There were three groups of people at this event ready to do their bidding of what they thought was right. The only difference in this event than what happen in Charlottesville, is there was a master teacher present, Jesus. He had one group of people with him in the Temple earnestly seeking to learn history from the true historian.

The other two groups approached the assembly with different objectives. Their plans were to violently stone this women for her actions. Make no mistake, had Jesus not been there all three groups would likely had participated in her murder. Their hearts were sincere but they were sincerely wrong.

They could see the problem with others but they couldn't see the problem with themselves. In this case, "Many Sides" were blinded to their need of a savior. And how did Jesus expose their vile hatred of their sister? He said, "He who is NOT guilty let him cast the first stone." And the scripture records that there was none left standing. Yes, "Many Sides" were wrong.

Sadly, people have lost their moral guide, the Bible, as to how to discern truth. People can't discern when they hear truth from a lie because they use CNN or FOX news as their litmus. Or, they use politicians as their moral guide. Instead, Christ and His Word should always be our guide. Here, Jesus sets the example. All of you are as guilty as this lady, if NOT, cast the first stone! It doesn't sound right when the President says it but he is exactly right. To think that anyone at this event has moral authority over the others is as Sinful as the hate that you think the other side possess. There were three sides that walked away. The people He was teaching, the Scribes and the Pharisees. Only the Savior and the sinner remained standing. And this is a good position to be in!! Repentant sinners are safe in His hands.

Another Take on The Confederate Flag:
"An abuse of a thing doesn't nullify its proper use."

Often, groups who take hard stances either for or against it call me to discuss the Confederate Flag. Honestly, I'm not a flagger and have stayed away from the dividing issue intentionally. My thought has been and continues to be to rather approach people where there is agreement. Christianity is that bridge which I stake every claim to be true, worthy and glorious to share. Discussing the Confederate Flag in my circles of Blacks and Whites, there is often no common ground.

Yet, I do have an official stance and I was reminded of it in a way that prompted me to share this post. I came across these words, "An abuse of a thing doesn't nullify its proper use." These words are from John Richards, Managing Director of The Billy Graham Center for Evangelicalism at Wheaton College. In his article, "Myth #3 Slavery and the White Man's Religion" dated January 8, 2017

Richards destroys the notion that Christianity was given to Blacks as a result of Slavery. In doing this, he doesn't nullify the Christian influence of Southerners. He simply goes a lot deeper into the matter to uncover more of the truth. I have always had an appreciation of history, including Church

History. In my appreciation of history, I'm often faced with talking to people who have only considered traditional perspectives on history. One of those traditional antidotal historical lessons that Black folks face when they matriculate through college is this: Christianity is the religion of white folks passed on to us from the institution of slavery. I once had to wrestle this claim. I remember several well-spoken Black activist friends of mine who thought it foolish to be Christian. I held to the faith. Or should I say, He held me to His faith.

Sadly. today many adult friends of mine tell me how their young Black men and women return home from College with the Blue-Eyed Devil Theology. This younger generation is buying the lie! On the surface, this argument can be persuasive to a young Black impressionable mind or even an old one. Considering the plight of African American communities, our history in this country, the lack of honest intellectual debate wrapped around a culture of being un-churched over the last twenty-thirty years and you can see the outcome. "It's the Whites man's religion!"

Nevertheless, as I grew in my love of God and my love of history, I came to understand that He is not void of using history for His glory. Forward 25 years later and the Confederate Flag was placed in the midst of my personal history. I am a descendant of a proud Black Confederate. Richards does a great job to point out that some of the most influential early Christians were Africans. He points to men of African Descent who were the early fathers of Christianity. Men like Origen, Tertullian, Augustine and Athanasius (All of these men were from parts of Africa). In fact, Northern Africans contributed greatly to the early infancy of Christianity. It is true that the Slave trade mostly included West Africa (With the exception of the Barbary Arab Slave Trade which included Northern Africa, Italy, Portugal, Spain, the Britain Islands, Iceland, The Netherlands, interior, East and South Africa-largely by Arabs of the Ottoman Empire) Moreover, Richards points to the Bible in Acts 2:10, 8:27, 11:20 as proof of early African Christian Influence. This is not hard to get your mind around if you view a map of the Mediterranean Sea. You realize that the sea, that is often referred to in the Bible that Jesus spent time on separates Northern Africa from Europe/Rome. This was the hub of early Christianity.

Moreover, it was these words of Richards that reminded me of a deeper truth.

"An abuse of a thing doesn't nullify its proper use." This is true of Christianity and this is true of anything else. Wrong doctrine leads to wrong living. The closer we move toward Christ (correct doctrine) throughout the annals of History, the closer we resemble and exist as God's Children. Yes, Christianity not rightly understood can be abused. Abusers may be sincere but can be sincerely wrong.

I think the same holds true of the Confederate Flag. It has been abused and abused in ways that are sincerely wrong. Yet, its abuse, does not nullify its proper use, no more than the abuse of Christianity nullifies the fact that Men of Africa had influence on the development of early Christianity. The fact that many Whites, even today, think that slavery was God's gift of Christianity to Blacks doesn't nullify the historical truths that Africans helped spread Christianity to a pagan world.

One of my favorites is Sextus Julius Africanus, year 160-year 240. Julius Africanus was a Christian Traveler, historian and writer. Some of his writings still exist. He is known to have heavily influenced early Christian Father, Eusebius and all early-late writers of Church history. The first Pope of African Birth was Pope Victor 1 (Papacy 189-199). The next Pope of African descent was Pope Miltiades (Papacy July 2, 311- January 10, 314). But it was Pope Gregory that launched the greatest Christian Reach into the Pagan world of Europe when he sent another African Brother, Augustine of Hippo (known as the Gregorian Missionaries or Augustinian Missionaries) to the Britannia Islands. King Edwin of Northrumbia was converted in 637. Christianity spread and these mostly Germanic Anglican Pagans would become known as puritans by 1560.

The Pilgrims (Puritans) who we celebrate during Thanksgiving and who received God's Grace from the early Roots of Christ Ministry by way of Africa came out of this church, The Church Of England.

So, what's the Crux of this matter? Here it is: "An abuse of a thing doesn't nullify its proper use." The fact that most Blacks may think that the Confederate Flag is a symbol of hate, because of the abuse it has endured by White supremacist, racist or those who defame its use, doesn't nullify the fact that thousands of Southerners see it as a symbol of heritage, faith and courage and honor. Nor does it nullify the fact that Blacks served this Flag with great honor and pride. Thus, if I can apply this principle of abuse and nullification to the truth of Christianity, how much more am I to apply it to a Flag? Thus, this is my stance on the Confederate Flag. Let it shine so that all may see and never forget those who died in the War Between the States. If we forget our history, we are doomed to repeat it. Let those who honor their dead do so with dignity and without shame. For there is no condemnation for those who are in Christ Jesus. Finally, when you consider history, it's too precious to destroy. God works through History. For some reason, He did it this way. For His Glory!!

Wow! A Black Woman on Monuments. She Understands the Opportunity at Hand.

So, wouldn't it be fitting to make our ancestors a part of our story? These were the words of a women who only ask the question, "Why not monuments for our ancestors placed side by side the Confederate monuments?" It would be a beautiful sight to see opposing organizations come together to reflect the different storylines of our history through monuments of art for generations to come. Her recommendation of putting the monuments side by side implies several things that are significant. For one, it's ok to allow Confederate monuments to stand. Secondly, it implies a cohesive effort of working together side by side as history is reflected through this effort. Finally, she places great value on the reality of the importance of Black men's stories. The likes of Nat Turner, Benjamin Banneker and others could offer a different perspective on history that allows the kind of dialogue that is necessary for reconciliation..

To this lady I write, you are thinking outside the box. Yes! Now, you are really on to something. I would love to see these organizations take on this project together. For every Confederate monument, let's put up one that represents the story of our people. You know who would help in this effort? The Confederate Southerners would give to this cause, provide space for such monuments. Now wouldn't that be beautiful?

The problem that we have is that no one wants to think outside the box. This lady gets it. I'm challenging everyone to think differently. I've already had someone say, "We got Monuments of Black folks." That's NOT what she said! She said, "Side by Side!" That means, we are together in the preservation of our heritages. Blacks and Whites! Southerners Unite! Educate our kids, leave a legacy for generations to explore. Through this effort, this generation will indicate a moment in time in which we came together to do this.

Destruction always lead to something more creative and more beautiful. Now is the time. This is the time for everyone to be creative and say, "We are going to construct a monument to Nat Turner and we are placing it right next to Robert E. Lee." This is so right, it's hilarious. But, this is the kind of thinking that we lack today because everyone wants to be 100% correct. "It's a my way or the high way era." Now, for all of those who think they hate being political correct. Go and encourage your group to take on something like this for the cause!

When Race Didn't Matter to Us in Mississippi

I recently attended my 30-year class reunion. What a joy to see old friends. My wife got a chance to see us reflect on the good ol' times we had together. I had one friend that wasn't able to make it to the reunion. Robert sustained a quadriplegic injury during the last week of our senior high school year. Just before graduation, a diving incident took his limbs away from him but it didn't take his heart. When I enrolled at Jackson State University that following Fall, I took a weekend job as a rehabilitation technician on the spinal cord injury floor of a large rehabilitation hospital in Jackson, MS. Little did I know, I would be helping to take care of my friend, Robert. After his rehabilitation, Robert went on to graduate from Mississippi State receiving his Master's degree and lived a productive life until several months ago.

I talked to my wife about Robert on the way to the reunion and again during the reunion. How he and I would swim together every summer at the city park in Tupelo. I shared with her his spirit of joy and perseverance and I was in awe that he had been in a wheelchair for thirty years and not once had I ever known him to complain. Instead of church the next morning, I told my wife that I wanted to go see my friend, Robert.

When we arrived at his room in the nursing facility, a sign greeted us, "I can do all things in Christ who strengthens me." I took him an audio copy of my book and he was glad to get it. Although, it had been years since I last saw him, Robert called my name the moment I walked through the door. It was a special time with this dear, sweet brother. What was more shocking to me was my wife's response when we got back in the car. She said, "the way you talked about him, I thought he was Black." I said to her, "I never said he was Black, I told you he was my friend." Believe it or not, in this little Mississippi town and for many years as we grew up, race didn't matter to us. We were friends and to this day, we still are!

Robert went to be with the Lord today! I am so happy for him. His body is restored and his joy is complete. It's amazing to me to think that one day he and I will swim together again. In thinking of this reunion, I can't help but to realize that he has already met my great-great grandfather and is able to share what testimony he has left for the world to behold. Christ is marvelous and I'm thankful He gave me one last visit with my friend on this side of heaven before he departed. I long to be in Heaven with all the saints. A place where race will truly not matter!!!

HERE IS WHAT HYPOCRISY LOOKS LIKE:

Jesse Hollan, Washington Journalist says:

"We as Americans build up a myth of our country, and a lot of times, we don't want to look behind that myth," he added. *"For me, finding out the truth and acknowledging the participation of everyone in the construction of this country just makes our country richer."*

Mrs. Obama was reaching for a similar point on Monday, emphasizing as her husband often does that the strengths of the United States spring in part from its ugly and painful past.

NEW YORK TIMES- "The White House That Slaves Helped Build" By JULIE HIRSCHFELD DAVIS July 26, 2016.

It can be TRUE on one hand that "the truth and acknowledging the participation of everyone in the construction of this country just makes our country richer" as long as you, the beholder, value what was constructed! If I said that my great-great grandfather was a Black Confederate and served Robert E. Lee as an orderly while a FREE Black man, these same people would say that I'm crazy. They will tear down the FLAG that he served proudly but then declare on the other hand that "our ugly and painful past" is the strength of the United States. REALLY? If that's the case, why do hypocrites continue to attack the great state of Mississippi and the State Flag? Can I not love my Confederate brother? Does love only flow one way? If the first lady can sleep in a house built by slaves, why can't I celebrate my Confederate heritage as a Black man without hesitation despite the ugly and painful past? This is the grace that God affords us. To love despite our past, not to hold the past against a people because they are southerners who honor their heritage and keep their flag.

If I am to honor the contributions of slaves who built the White house, how much more am I to honor the work of a free Black man who served in the Confederate armies? Does the White House not have the stains of blood of slaves on its walls? Why does the Confederate southerner have to give up his heritage and his flag to be loved?

Why does America continue to spew its venomous poison on everything that is southern and Confederate? At the same time, we are promoting love to all kinds of people, genders and celebrating a house built by slaves, we are trashing the southern Confederate. Why not take down the house? No, we waddle in our hypocrisy and celebrate the contributions of slaves when it is fitting and acceptable to us. When we don't understand the contributions of slaves, we want to destroy the aspect that we do not know or cannot comprehend. It's a slippery slope. In theory and in practice, I agree with the statement, "We are richer as a country when we acknowledge the participation of everyone." That's exactly why I wrote the book, *Robert E. Lee's Orderly A Modern Black Man's Confederate Journey.* Black folks have been at the forefront of history including participating in the Confederate armies. I don't claim to understand it all, but I am just as proud of my great-great grandfather, Turner Hall, Jr. as the First Lady is to wake up in a house built by slaves.

Let me clarify one thing. I am not calling the First Lady a hypocrite, although she probably didn't mind the insult to the Flag of Mississippi being treated like it was no more than a floor rag. Even as a Black man in the south, I will be honest and say that it made me mad. No, I respect and love the First Lady. I just want the same respect and love for my dear Confederate brothers and sisters in the South! Stop trying to shame people about the past! God never did that! No, you hypocrites! Christ said, "He who is not guilty, let him cast the first stone." And none did!

Genealogy

So many people ask, "What's the big deal, Al, about your genealogy?" I've had a lot of time to think about this. I realize that many people are insensitive to genealogy. They couldn't care less who their ancestors were. In fact, many people don't understand why so many people care about "those old, dead people that you never knew anyway." I can't tell you how many times I've heard these claims. If you add Confederate ancestry/genealogy to this you will get even more dismayed. After all, "They lost the War, let's just forget about those old, grey guys! They don't count!" Yet, I want to bring this point to the table. There are over three thousand people in the Bible who have some aspect of genealogy listed. Genealogy is important. I can say that with confidence because I see it clearly throughout the Bible.

Example of Biblical genealogy:

From Adam to Abraham 1 Chronicles 1

Adam, Seth, Enosh; Kenan, Mahalalel, Jared; Enoch, Methuselah, Lamech; Noah, Shem, Ham, and Japheth.

The sons of Japheth: Gomer, Magog, Madai, Javan, Tubal, Meshech, and Tiras. The sons of Gomer: Ashkenaz, Riphath, and Togarmah. The sons of Javan: Elishah, Tarshish, Kittim, and Rodanim.

The sons of Ham: Cush, Egypt, Put, and Canaan. The sons of Cush: Seba, Havilah, Sabta,

Raama, and Sabteca. The sons of Raamah: Sheba and Dedan. 10 Cush fathered Nimrod. He was the first on earth to be a mighty man.

(The rest of Chronicles is filled with genealogy)

Now, why would GOD choose to have such genealogical recordings in His Word? Have you ever thought about that? Probably one of the most preached genealogical characters in the Bible is found in vs 10 above (Nimrod). For some reason God sees that he is pointed out to be the "first on earth to be a mighty man." I guess, if you feel like a lot of people do about genealogy, this is just ol' grey men that should be forgotten. Yet, the fact that they are in the Word of God speaks to their importance to His story and the fact that He honors history. It is His. They will not be forgotten by the mere fact that God Himself wrote their names in His book.

So, if I were to write out my genealogy including all the details of every birth somewhere in that line there would be a pause, from my perspective, that would say "And he fathered Turner Hall, Jr. and Turner was with the Confederate Giants, Lee and Forrest!!!" Now, that's something that I would take note of, even today! Let's celebrate genealogy. God certainly valued it and I don't think He covered it up. Nor was He ashamed to include Rahab, the prostitute, in the genealogy of Jesus. His beloved Son was from the lineage of a prostitute!! What is that about? You may not care about your ancestors but I certainly care about mine!!!

Arnold & Elliott Family Rules

Always be honest (Proverbs 12:22)

Count your blessings (Psalms 34:1–3)

Forgive and forget (Micah 7:18)

Be supportive of one another (Acts 20:35)

Be kind and tenderhearted (Ephesians 4:32)

Keep your promises (Romans 4:21)

Comfort one another (1 Thessalonians 4:18)

And above all:
Love one another (Peter 1:22)

In Honor of my ancestors:

Great-Great-Grandparents
Turner Hall, Jr. & Francis Dilworth Hall
Lucian "Paw Dick" Arnold & Momma Jossie

Great Grandparents
Bennie Elliott and Mama Will

Grand Parents
Lucian "Ras" Arnold and Arine Elliott Arnold

About the Author: Al Arnold

I am a native-born Mississippian. I am African American. I am a Christian. I am a Husband. I am a father of two boys and one girl. I am a Southerner. Thanks to an ancestry.com DNA test, I can be a little more specific. Eighty-four percent of my DNA is from Africa. Fifteen percent of my DNA is from Europe. The remaining one percent is of West Asian descent. My ancestral roots are largely from Nigeria and Scandinavia (Sweden, Norway, and Denmark) with trace roots from West Africa and West Europe. It is estimated that over 3.5 million slaves were transported to the Americas from Nigeria during the slave trade. It is estimated that over two million Scandinavians immigrated to America between 1820 and 1920. Somewhere in the beautiful and yet ugly mix of things, my African ancestry mixed with my

Viking ancestry and I am who I am today by the Grace of God.

I am a descendent of a proud Black Confederate and a former slave. It is in this Grace that I have come to appreciate all of whom I am and all of whom others are. If they belong to the family of God through Christ, I am all the more compelled to love them. If they do not belong to the family of God through Christ, I am all the more compelled to love them.

alarnold@orderlyforlee.com
www.orderlyforlee.com
Facebook: orderlyforlee
Please Review Book at Goodreads.com or Amazon.com

Me and a few of my new found brothers and sister.
Connected at the Cross in Love.

Me and my Mississippi brother, Luckie McDonald.

Me and my Tennessee brother, Mike Cross.

Me and my Louisiana brother, Randy Jarreau.

Me and my Texas brother, Gary Bray.

Me and my brother from Florida, Robert Snead

Me and my brother from Georgia, Scott Gilbert, Jr.

Me and my Southern Sister from Alabama, Chantelle Brownlow.

A Black and White letter to the Church Part 1
"Thou Shalt Love Thy Neighbor As Thyself"

Mark 12: 31

As a Christian, it burdens me to witness other Christians use guilt as a tool to convey the reason for the removal of the State flag or Confederate monuments. And for those White Christians who fall for this scheme, I say hold onto your guilt, if you must, but the scriptures clearly teach there is NO condemnation for those who are in Christ Jesus. There is freedom whenever people turn to Christ (Free to be Jew or Gentile). Stop and think about that for a moment. Maybe you don't understand just how OFFENSIVE the Gospel is?

This message is thousand times more offensive than a flag or monument. For a JEW to accept a GENTILE? Really, God?

We are free indeed! Scriptures also clearly teach that the sins of the fathers are NOT transferable to their children in this regard. I am Mississippi born and raised. This is my home and no one loves this Great State more than I do.

What breaks my heart is not a state flag but senseless acts of violence that frequent our communities. I don't have to mention the recent pain felt when one of our youngest (A six-year-old) was brutally killed causing tears among Whites and Blacks all across this state. The outcry and pain that African Americans should have would be better served if it was over the shed blood of our children who die in the streets without reason or cause.

My Christian brothers are not all Black. They are Southerners who just happen to have a Confederate ancestor or in many cases many Confederate ancestors. Who among the Black community is calling their White Confederate brothers and sisters in Christ to sit down at their table and break bread with them?

Martin Luther King Jr. said it best when he said, " one day the son of the slave owner and the son of the slave will sit together at the table of brotherly love. Well, for me, that day has come!

There is nothing in this Dream to suggest that we would be disconnected from our heritage. In fact, when in Christ, we are afforded all the difference in the world. He calls us to love. He doesn't call all to be the same in all regards. Be ye like minded as one is not a call to a singleness of mind about our past more so than a singleness of mind of who we are as believers in Christ. And as believers, we are called toward each other in our individual likeness. We are not called to lay down our uniqueness. He called the Jew and the Gentile to Himself. He didn't call them from themselves in that they had to deny who they were as a people group to be accepted by the other. Quite the opposite. Yet, like political flunkies, we are tossed to and fro by every wind of what is politically correct and feels good to the flesh.

Jesus did something much greater. He told Peter, "Do not call anything that I have made clean, unclean." Well, I'm here to say that I don't understand why He did it but He did it. There will be those who are Confederates in heaven too.

Rednecks are included in the fold of God. Yes, the ones you despise because they hold onto a part of who God made them. Grace is sufficient for them also. Once I came to embrace this understanding of God's Grace, I had but one challenge. To love my brother despite his love for his heritage and his Confederate flag. It would be much easier to love people who are just like me.

God knew this as well. He didn't give me an easy path but He is the one from the foundation of the world laid out His path for me. So, what did he do? He revealed to me an ancestor who was a proud Confederate.

My great-great grandfather, Pappa Turner, served in the Confederate armies for four years. And Pappa Turner was no distant relative far from my memory. Here me when I say, I knew about Him as a young child. My grandmother kept him before us as a beacon of hope for our generation to model. She was as proud of her grandfather as any man is today of theirs. So, when God showed me the depth of who this man was, he also gave me a love for the people that I once despised. It's as if he said, you will become one with them as I am with you to demonstrate my revealed Grace.

This journey has not been easy but it certainly has been fun trusting and obeying God to take up a love for a people that look nothing like me, talk nothing like me but is as much as me as any. Not only was my ancestor an orderly for Robert E. Lee, he was a slave to Confederate General Nathan Bedford Forrest. It was like God screaming to me, I will not do this quietly Al. That my name may be known and that my Grace be proven to be sufficient for the worst, I will show you how boldly I have done this from the foundation of the world that you may stand with your Southern White brothers and show them and the world the love that I have for all of those who are called by my name. Who am I to argue with God?

Furthermore, as a Black man, I've always wanted to see monuments and the Confederate flag. They always reminded me of the things I didn't like. What man wants to only see things that he loves. Show me that man and I will show you a man who forgoes reflections in life that are meant to make him a whole being. I understand so well now, how and why Jesus hung out in some of the most unexpected places. It is in these places that His Grace abounds so greatly and His love is so perfecting. One of the problems with appealing to this flag issue solely on the basis of race and not on the faith claims of Christ is that race alone invites those into the matter that are not of Christ. To mix the two will always fall to the side of humanism. That ugly enemy of the Cross that attempts to pit one man's past failures over the others. This results in the use of guilt as a means of shaming people into some measure of righteousness. The dirty little secret is this. There is none who is not culpable before a Holy and righteous God. We all have sinned and fallen short of God's Grace. Removing symbols of history or symbols that are dear to my White brothers because of their past, makes me no more righteous than anyone.

And yet, I find that my ancestor was just as proud of that flag and celebrated his Confederate service, as a slave, just like all Confederates until the day he died in 1942. Not only did he travel to New York City to interview on a National Talk Radio show as a Black Confederate, he received the honor of being the most distinguished citizen by Blacks and Whites in his community for his service to General Robert E. Lee. I'm tired of Mississippi bashing! I also don't want to live in a society that threatens to take every single symbol of history away just because people may have differences about it.

Furthermore, God didn't tell us not to be different or even not to think different about social issues. He told us to "Love one another as yourself." So, for every cry to take down a Confederate flag to show love for a Black brother in Christ, how about putting one up one for that White brother in Christ. And let he who is not guilty cast the first stone. We have enough stone casters from outside this state. It's time to allow the Grace of God to demonstrate a love that surpasses understanding and that is where I stand. It doesn't mean or suggests that the

Confederate flag was never used for ill will. Nor does it suggest I support slavery. Those issues are covered in the Grace of God and I am free to love my brothers! There are thousands of Christians throughout the South who honor that flag as a rightful demonstration of their heritage or history. They should be able to do so without being lumped in with all the wickedness of history as if they are the only debtors to God's Grace.

Quite honestly, I am tickled pink how God and only God could have entrusted me with this opportunity. To be blessed to write a story that tells people about His Amazing Grace has been one of the most exciting things. Speaking of "Amazing Grace," that beautiful song was given to the Church by God at the hand of a slave trader, John Newton. Newton didn't stop trading slaves when he pinned this beautiful hymn. It took seven years for his sanctification to catch up with his Salvation before he put down that horrific trade. Are we going to remove this hymn that God gave the church because it came to us at the bloody, filthy hands of a slave trader? Absolutely not!

Yet, if we use the measure of offense that people call for today as a means to remove everything that is offensive, this hymn could never be heard again in a single Black church. In fact, I too beg but I beg of my Black brothers. I beg you, in the name of Christ, to stop singing this hymn in your church until you go find a son of a slave owner and eat at his table. Break bread with him. Go seek him out and find that you are as one. Can you imagine a Black church without the hymn, "Amazing Grace?" No, you can't. It would be a tragedy. Well, I simply cannot imagine a South that is not allowed to hold to all of who God has made it be. There is no cry for that among Black Christians. Instead, we sing this White European spiritual song every Sunday in our Churches and at every Black Funeral. It is one of many Negro spiritual songs that can be played on the piano by using only the Black keys of the piano in what is historically known as the musical slave scales. It is without hesitation, our song of choice as that which tells our story and share our hope in our Lord and Savior. This is our heritage and we dare not let it go. Yet, we scoff at our brothers who desire to hold to theirs? We have swallowed a camel and are choking on gnats!

Connected at the Cross in Love,
Al Arnold, this 1st day of October,
In the Year of Our Lord 2017.

A Black and White letter to the Church Part 2 "Thou Shalt Love Thy Neighbor as Thyself" Mark 12: 31

To my dear White Southern brothers and sisters in Christ, perhaps no greater enemy has besieged you since the eve of the Great War Between the States. Your territory has indeed been invaded externally and internally by those who seek to erase your heritage altogether, if nothing else, from public view. You are faced with daunting odds and an insurmountable task. However, you have yet to fully employ the greatest weapon of warfare given to mankind, love! Love your enemies and pray for those who persecute you so that you may prove your sonship to your Father in heaven. Perhaps you will win some battles in the courts but only until the courts reverse their decision down the road. Perhaps you will shout louder than your foes in protest but only until you die out and your shouting becomes a distant memory of the past. You may even prove winsome with education until you realize that even education breeds the greatest fools among us. But this weapon of Love, it has the power that surpasses all understanding. It is the greatest weapon that Christ has given us.

Historically, there are a few well-known men who truly demonstrated they understood this weapon. More importantly, they had the courage and faith to implement it against the greatest odds. Christ, when he said, "Father, forgive them for they know not what they do." Because of His love, the Christian Symbol is forever edged into the hearts and minds of the world. A symbol that once was the scorn of the earth, is now that which helps to sustain humanity, establish its precepts and guide its men toward higher and higher depths of peace with one another.

Martin Luther King Jr. knew this concept well. He used love through mass organized nonviolent marches and changed the world by agreeing to use Love instead of hate. Gandhi, though not a Christian, understood this great power. Love is unique in that it is not a trait limited to Christians. Yet, it is one of the highest commands to the Christian and should be one of their highest banners. Unfortunately, it is not. We are so busy judging our brothers, we don't seize the opportunities that God gives us to unite with him. This current acute failure to recognize and see these opportunities are primarily due to the division that our two party political system has caused in this country. Let me give you an example of this from the depths of my heart.

When so many Young Black men were tragically killed during the last several years the whole of Christendom in the Confederate nation had a great opportunity to witness for Christ by joining their Black brothers and sisters in a movement for peace between the races. It would not have necessarily provided peace within the African American Community but what witness for Christ and your cause could have been shown had you seized this opportunity instead of ridiculing it on every end? Can you imagine what would have happened if a thousand white men with Confederate attire showed up at a Black lives matter movement with the intent to say, "Yes, Black lives do matter, brothers and sisters and we are going to join you in this cry! We will join you as Christians, although Southern and White, we love you and we hurt because you hurt. It's ok to say, "we don't agree with everything or even understand everything, but we will stand with you in Christ." Now, that's about as crazy as a Black person being in support of a Confederate flag in

2017. Yet, that's exactly what this kind of love will cause you to do. It takes the great risk of being misunderstood. It fears not! It's Agape Love.

How can it be that my Southern White brothers and sisters can respect a Black man who is not politically correct when it comes to honoring his Confederate heritage against the tide of what is so clearly an overwhelming sea of contempt? Yet, when the tide is changed or the shoe is put on the other foot, as they say, my White brothers and sisters find that their political correctness is just as damaging as everyone else's. They too fall to the political correctness of the day as it would be wholly politically incorrect for them to voice support for any movement that is outside of the sphere of their core constituents.

Political correctness says there must be two opposing forces at all times! A North and a South. A Black and a White. A Right and a Left. And these forces listen only to their Captains. Many, who are marginal Christians, if Christian at all.

Thus, a man must choose between Black lives and Blue lives. And the folly continues to divide and conquer. It becomes politically incorrect for the White man to march for Black lives and it becomes politically incorrect for the Black man to march for blue lives. And this is the trap that awaits all of us. The many schemes of the real enemy that keeps us at each other's throats and separated across divided lines. Instead, we should be rising up as a great Christian army in support of our men whether they are black, blue or white.

Gandhi said, "An eye for an eye, only makes the whole world go blind." As long as this eye for and eye mentality dominates our society, Americans will continue to destroy each other, fall to hatred, bitterness, and unforgiveness. Our society will continue to degrade toward the abyss as the judgment of God goes out against men for failing to "Love your neighbor as yourself." Let's imagine a society where it would be perfectly acceptable for a white Confederate heritage flag toting Rebel to yell out, "Black Lives Matter," and fear no retribution from his fellow compatriots and no disdain from his Black brother. In return, imagine that same Black brother saying, "Rebel, you may yell! Your yell is not mine but I can respect and love you because you are my brother!" Then, the enemy falls to his knees and beg us to go back to hating each other. And perhaps the non-Christian falls to his knees in complete confusion as the love of Christ weakens him to a state of repentance! Agape love is a radical love that has this kind of power. It's a love that is for the unlovely and unworthy, the others! It's the kind of love that defies the norms. It makes no sense to the casual observer. But more importantly, it is commanded of us. This is the love that God used to sacrifice His Righteous Son for sinners. You see, it is truly a stumbling stone and many men trip over it.

There are many quotes by Robert Edward Lee that helps me to understand that he too knew this kind of love very well. Perhaps there is no one of more noble character, by the fate of history, whose shadow has been hidden under clouds of doubt. Had he chosen to fight for the North, he, instead of Grant, would have been President of the United States after the Civil War. Lee stated, "What a cruel thing war is... to fill our hearts with hatred instead of love for our neighbors." Moreover, he quoted, "I have fought against the people of the North because I believed they were seeking to wrest from the South its dearest rights. But I have never cherished toward them bitter or vindictive feelings, and I have never seen the day when I did not pray for them." Lee's understanding of the high command to love your neighbor and to pray for your enemies was foremost on his mind throughout the war. In fact, it was his great love for his neighbor that caused him to deny the military offer from Lincoln as he could not bear the thought of taking up arms against his native Virginians. But what kind of man goes to war and declares no vindictive or bitter feelings toward his enemies?

Who actually prays for his enemies daily while simultaneously defending himself from that enemy during the cruelties of war? Only a man who clearly understands what it means to love.

Lee is one of those great men, like the early church father, Polycarp, called to "play the man" as God conducted His business for the ages. I must say, God knows His business and His people and He chose Lee for such a time as this. I think it wouldn't matter to Lee what is remembered of him for he was a humble man.

Men of his stature always seem to understand the crux of the matter. In his case, it was love. In our day, it remains the same! Who among you has the capacity to truly love? Yet, like all men of his great stature, he is worthy to be remembered. I think one of his greatest statements of love was his willingness to lose all and to bare all in suffering that slavery is abolished. Lee stated, "So far from engaging in a war to perpetuate slavery, I rejoice that slavery is abolished. I believe it will be greatly for the interests of the South. So fully am I satisfied of this, as regards Virginia especially, that I would cheerfully have lost all I have lost by the war, and have suffered all I have suffered, to have this object attained." Here is a brother who was willing to lay down his life that others may obtain theirs. This is what Agape love looks like.

Agape love is the one lasting trait that ascends this earth into the next life with those who have been captured by its grace through Christ. Faith, Hope, and Love and the greatest of these is Love. Why is love the greatest? Because faith and hope will cease to be once we cross over and see the end of our faith and finally realize the reason for our hope. But love will never cease as we come into the presence of eternal love and experience its fullness beholding Him face to face. Simply put, if we can't love those who we see every day, how can we love Him who we cannot see?

Brothers and sisters, you must love despite the gnashing of teeth and the gouging of history that affronts you. There is no worse outcome than for those who are attacked to become bitter and vindictive. Christ, Martin Luther King Jr., Gandhi, Mandela and Robert E. Lee all understood this, love thy neighbor as thyself!

Connected at the Cross in Love,
Al Arnold, this 1st day of October,
In the Year of Our Lord 2017.

The Southern Inheritance The South Has Risen!

"Behold how good and pleasant it is that brothers dwell together in unity!" (Psalm 133 a)

The real beauty of unity is brighter and more apparent to the eye when there has been the greatest disharmony. The greater the divide, the greater the joy of unity is displayed. Unity is our Southern jewel, if only we would turn to it.

A rich inheritance has been given to the South. We have a mixed culture and shared heritage knitted together historically by circumstances and its people at the hand of a gracious God. This inheritance resonates from our proximity to one another over time, our understanding of family and its extensions, an appreciation of the uniqueness of our culinary expressions and our common values of faith and hard work. The New South is rooted in the Old South. They cannot be separated no more than sin can be separated from the Cross. Sin affords us the Cross and without it there would be no need for Redemption. Because of sin, we are always in need of being found daily at the Cross.

We are debtors. Southerners are indebted to the past and to the future of the South. To see it any other way would tread heavily and shamefully on the backs of those who gave us the pathways to oneness. Although some did not see it or ever imagine its glory, the South has gloriously risen. We have risen to be the shining example of the richness in diversity and unity that is misunderstood by outsiders.

To the shock of many who travel through this glorious land, there is a people who honors, respects and shares in daily experiences for the good of all. We are Children of a living God. He has mysteriously done what only He could have done and continues to do; He makes us one in Him. What a blessed inheritance we have received. This is not despite our past; it is because of our past that we have such blessed hope of unity. Turn to that inheritance my Southern brothers and sisters, for in Christ, we are all one people!

Aunt Ruth's Down Home Tea Cakes

Ingre dients and Instructions

- **5 & ½ Cups of Flour**
- **2 Cups of Sugar**
- **2 & ½ sticks of butter**
- **3 Teaspoons of Baking Powder**
- **1 Teaspoon of Baking soda**
- **¼ cup of Buttermilk**
- **3 Eggs**
- **2 Teaspoons of pure vanilla or your choice**
- ***Instructions: Place all Ingredients in a mixing bowl. Knead well. Roll out into the cookie size of your choice. Bake in a preheated oven for 12 minutes at 350 degrees.***

Papa Turner's oldest living grandchild, Aunt Ruth (95) loves to bake her Tea Cakes for the Family.

A Southern Treat

Mama's Whipping Cream Pound Cake

Ingre dients and Instructions

- **6 Eggs**
- **3 Cup of Sugar**
- **3 Cups of Cake Flour**
- **½ Pint of whipping cream**
- **2 sticks of butter (½ lbs)**
- **1 TBS of vanilla flavor**
- **1 TBS of butternut flavor**
- *Instructions: Cream sugar and butter until smoot. Add eggs slowly one at a time, mixing well after each one. Add flour alternating with the whipping cream. Add flavor and blend well. Pour batter into a greased bunt or tube pan. Place in a cold oven and bake at 325 for 1hr 15 min.*

Every time you visited Mama's house there was something to eat. One of her specialties was the Whipping Cream Pound Cake. Bake and Enjoy! A Daily Treat. Welcome Home!

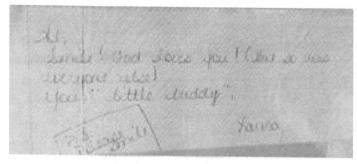

Me and Laura thirty years later!
And a 30-year-old love note that reminds me to smile!

At the gate to the Whitehouse with my Confederate
brother, Robert Jackson.

Al in the Whitehouse Press Room. "I'm telling my Confederate story to the World while smiling God's love. No more sad days

Me and my wife at Gettysburg November, 2016

Cousin Troy Lee gave me my first lesson in genealogy. (9/25/1936-6/18/2007)

Me and my sisters, brothers, children,
nieces and nephews with Dad and Aunt
Ruth.

The Arnold family. In the middle is Aunt Pearl, family
historian and glue that holds the family.

Mr. B. Turner Hall & Florine Hall.
"Boy, that flag is ours!"

Forever pardoned, the West Wing Black
Squirrel that welcomed us to the Whitehouse.

Women, the backbone of the family. Aunt Avis and
Aunt Pearl holding up their big brother, uncle
Gene. Family Reunion, 2016.

Family support and encouragement
presented at the 2016 annual family reunion.